The Contemporary Novel in German

A SYMPOSIUM

The Contemporary Novel in German

▭▭▭▭▭▭▭▭▭▭▭▭▭▭▭▭▭▭▭▭▭▭▭▭▭▭▭▭▭▭▭▭▭▭▭▭

A SYMPOSIUM

Edited with an Introduction by

Robert R. Heitner

Published for the
DEPARTMENT OF GERMANIC LANGUAGES OF The University of Texas by the
UNIVERSITY OF TEXAS PRESS, Austin and London

Standard Book Number 292–73670–3
Library of Congress Catalog Card No. 67–25327
Copyright © 1967 by the University of Texas Press
All Rights Reserved

Manufactured in the United States of America

Second Printing, 1969

Contents

Introduction ——————————————————————————————— 1
   ROBERT R. HEITNER

Perspective and Dualism in the Novels of Böll ——————— 9
   WALTER HERBERT SOKEL

Heimito von Doderer's *Demons* and the Modern Kakanian
Novel ——————————————————————————————————— 37
   HEINZ POLITZER

The Present Quandary of German Novelists ——————— 63
   GERD GAISER

The Search for Self, Inner Freedom, and Relatedness in the
Novels of Max Frisch ——————————————————————— 91
   CHARLES W. HOFFMANN

Günter Grass: The Artist as Satirist ———————————115
   HENRY HATFIELD

Notes on the Contributors ———————————————————135

Index ————————————————————————————————137

Introduction

BY ROBERT R. HEITNER

University of Illinois at Chicago Circle

The five essays in this book were originally presented as lectures at the seventh annual symposium held at The University of Texas, on November 29 and 30, and December 1, 1965, under the sponsorship of the Department of Germanic Languages. The authors include four professors of German at American universities and one practicing German novelist, Gerd Gaiser, who was prevented by a sudden illness from attending the symposium and giving his lecture in person. Illness also kept Professor Heinz Politzer from reading his own paper. In spite of these unfortunate absences, the symposium proceeded according to its appointed schedule. All five lectures were read to the audience and were discussed afterwards, the discussions being led by the invited observers, Professors Robert L. Kahn, A. Leslie Willson, Gerd Hillen, and George A. Jocums.

In its theme the symposium was very broad; in actual scope, of course, it had to be limited to just a few novelists and novels. Two prominent and widely acclaimed German authors, Heinrich Böll and Günter Grass, were selected for close study and detailed interpretation, as were one Swiss author, Max Frisch, and one Austrian, Heimito von Doderer. Placed in the center of these four individual treatments—as also in this volume—Dr. Gerd Gaiser's comprehensive remarks about the state of novel-writing in the German language today served as a consolidating nexus. In the discussions, as might be expected, many other novels and novelists came into mention.

Professor Sokel's perceptive analysis of the novels of Heinrich Böll stresses the constant theme of alienation in them, that is, the inability of persons who resisted the Nazi evil before and during the war to take an active and positive role in the reconstruction of Germany after the war—or, stated more universally, the inability of honest, sincere persons of good will to make their mark and prevail against the graceless, dishonest, self-seekers at any time, in any place. A moral victory, nevertheless, is reserved for the sympathetic characters in their steadfast refusal to relinquish their ideals. An almost classical, Schillerian attitude, it might be said, but with a kind of weary stubbornness substituted for heroism, fanfare, and pathos.

Through intensive scrutiny of one of Heimito von Doderer's novels, *Die Dämonen*, Professor Politzer furnishes an interpretation of style and viewpoint valid for all of the Austrian author's works. It is the unique atmosphere of the former Habsburg lands, of "Kakania," that Doderer vividly captures in his rich, lengthy narrative, a "total novel," characterized by an inexhaustible supply of personages, episodes, and factual details and by an omnipresent—if not omniscient—narrator. In the evocation of Doderer's own specific environment nothing is limited or provincial, despite the fact that a street plan of Vienna is a necessary aid for clear understanding of some of the action. A parallel to Böll's pessimistic demonstration of the defeat of good men by evil men may be seen in Doderer's description of the extinction of Austrian freedom through absurd mob actions and the burning of the Vienna Palace of Justice. A degree of hopefulness and confidence can be detected in Doderer's feeling that, after all, the "first reality," order and decency, has greater permanence than the "second reality," violence and demonic deeds.

Professor Hoffmann's illuminating discussion of the novels of Max Frisch centers on the special problem of identity-seeking, which is inherent to the prose fiction of this Swiss author. The struggle to understand himself is shown as the prime concern of each of Frisch's heroes—Stiller, Faber, and "Gantenbein"— and this struggle is carried on in the form of introspective reminiscing or (in the case of "Gantenbein") through the positing of a series of hypothetical selves. Through their search for identity these individuals also make a halting step toward the achievement of inner freedom and of meaningful relationships with other human beings. Each of the novels is a showcase for Frisch's mastery of psychological observation and insight; and in each the author's evident conviction that love is the essential key to happiness subtly comes to the fore.

In the novelistic works of Günter Grass, Professor Hatfield finds essentially a satirical purpose. He concludes that satire, in Grass's view, is the really important product of modern art. Grotesque little Oskar in *Die Blechtrommel*, standing apart from humankind because of his abnormality and yet in a position to pronounce judgment on normal folk, may well represent the artist type. He is the enemy of sham and corruption and of everything connected with Nazism (like the good persons in Böll's novels). His weapon against the things he hates is ridicule. Only in the maintenance of his own integrity, however, does Oskar win; he retires from the busy world of postwar Germany and—again like Böll's characters—cannot take part in its activity. The satire in *Hundejahre*, Professor Hatfield believes, is harsher than in *Die Blechtrommel*, with a tendency toward occasional heavyhandedness. Yet this latest novel displays a virtuosity of style so impressive as to insure its position as a major work of literature.

Dr. Gerd Gaiser, well-known author of the novels *Eine Stimme hebt an* (1950), *Die sterbende Jagd* (1953), *Das Schiff im Berg* (1955), and *Schlußball* (1958), as well as numerous short stories, contributes a succinct but remarkably comprehensive account[1] of the background history and the distinguishing features of the contemporary novel. He thereby indicates how precisely familiar the present-day German novelist is with the past development of the genre, the influences active upon it, and the "crisis" it is said to be undergoing. From Dr. Gaiser's paper it becomes clear that the serious novelist, however modestly he may disclaim the pretension, *is* likely to be a literary historian and critic in addition to being a creative writer. He does not work in an artistic vacuum, or entirely according to the inclinations of his heart and the promptings of his talent; he keeps abreast of literary developments and theories and is aware of how these may affect his own work.

Although viewed from different and highly original perspectives in these five essays, the contemporary novel in German

[1] Dr. Gaiser's lecture was written and read in German for the symposium, but has been translated into English for this volume by the editor.

6 — Robert R. Heitner

emerges from them, the reader will no doubt sense, with a unified, definite, almost simple character. Contemporary authors, successful in their rebellion against conventional form, plot, and characterization, have created, thanks to common influences and reciprocal imitation, a new, recognizable conformity—one might say a conventional unconventionality. Plot and character development retreat to the background, are hidden, or even completely disappear in the new type of novel. Everything suggestive of romantic imagination, adventure, and artificiality is foreign to it. Instead, endless attempts to portray the complexity and perplexity of modern life and endless fascination with the social and psychological prehistory, history, and aftermath of World War II (overtones of this also in the Swiss novels) typify the contents of the new novels. An intense, relentless preoccupation with reality, in all its aspects, has taken hold of the authors. Every scene, every word conveys a sense of the actual, the observed, the experienced—however erratic and eccentric the linguistic and stylistic means employed may be. The art of the novelist seems to consist in his ability to relay to the reader detail after detail of circumstances he himself is intimately familiar with and aware of—*conscious* of, would be the preferred term—and to do this in a consistently striking, compelling manner; for often, little suspense is provided to carry the reader along. What is said of the character Haseloff in Grass's *Hundejahre* can be said of these contemporary writers: "Er ist wirklich ein komischer Kerl und schreibt tausend Einzelheiten, die anderen nicht auffallen." [2] The *Weltanschauung* of the new novelists, insofar as it is distinguishable, also appears fairly homogeneous: existentialist, skeptical, ironic.

As Dr. Gaiser indicates in his essay, another unifying feature is the pervading emphasis on the dark and seamy sides of existence. His concern about what he considers to be an overemphasis and exaggeration in this regard may herald a new novel of his own combatting the trend; or it may reflect a more widespread, growing uneasiness which will lead eventually to a less depressing

[2] Günter Grass, *Hundejahre* (Berlin: Luchterhand, 1963), p. 329. "He is really an odd fellow and writes a thousand details that other people miss."

tone in the novels emanating from the German *Sprachraum.* Perhaps such a new tone is already discernible in Max Frisch's *Mein Name sei Gantenbein.*

Perspective and Dualism in the Novels of Böll

BY WALTER HERBERT SOKEL

Stanford University

Events in Böll's novels are presented from the perspective of alienated characters through whose minds and eyes we view the German scene. Böll undoubtedly learned from the American successors of Joyce and of Gertrude Stein. Hemingway, Thomas Wolfe, and Faulkner are influences, direct and indirect, on the form of his narratives. Böll eliminates the omniscient comment of the authorial voice and presents all situations and events through the sense impressions, memory, and reflections of his characters. At times he approaches the stream of consciousness.

Böll's earliest novels dealing with postwar Germany—*Und sagte kein einziges Wort* (1953) and *Haus ohne Hüter* (1954)— present a world in which the determining force of events seems to be material and economic. In naturalistic fashion, environment and circumstances seem to determine human actions and fate. In specific terms, the material and social consequences of the lost war apparently mould human life in Böll's postwar Germany. Overcrowding in the ruined cities ostensibly causes the tragic breakup of a marriage in *Und sagte kein einziges Wort*. His mother's poverty imposes a succession of spurious "uncles" on young Heinrich Briesach in *Haus ohne Hüter*. Frau Briesach, still a young woman in years, views the bleak prospect of a lonely and loveless future because she is unable to pay the costs of a denture. The threat of the premature loss of her teeth is in turn a consequence of the nutritional deprivations of the war years.

The structure of *Haus ohne Hüter* seems to reinforce the naturalistic view of human destiny as determined by socioeconomic circumstances. The novel consists largely of five alternating perspectives on a postwar German city. Two war widows and the only child of each provide four of these perspectives. One of the widows is the daughter of a wealthy manufacturer, the other's husband was an auto mechanic. Both families are victims of war; yet the victimizations of each differ considerably because of different economic and social situations. Orphanhood appears different to Heinrich, son of the worker, than to Martin, child of a prosperous upper-bourgeois home. Even though they appear different in many respects, however, in essence the problems of both widows and both orphans are alike. Each must come to grips with life deprived of its center, life without help, comfort, and completeness. This parallelism of perspectives of human deprivation in two widely different economic strata makes us suspect that the naturalistic interpretation may be less than adequate.

In one passage of the novel Böll makes the socioeconomic interpretation of the novel's events give way to a moral evaluation. The shift takes place literally and explicitly before the reader's eyes. Young Heinrich Briesach considers his mother's love life and the succession of "uncles" it imposes upon him. Why doesn't she get married, he wonders. The first answer that presents itself to him is the loss of her government pension in case of remarriage. That answer, however, proves to be inadequate as Heinrich reflects further. The example of a neighbor woman refutes the first answer. This neighbor, also a war widow and economically not better off than his mother, gave up her pension to marry the man she loved. Heinrich likewise considers his friend Martin's mother, who, though rich and not in need of a pension, does not remarry. Something other than economic factors must obviously be the answer to Heinrich Briesach's question. The neighbor did get married, forfeiting her pension, because she refused to sin; in other respects, too, she is shown as a pious, God-fearing woman. On a more complex, less explicit plane, it is as a moral being that Martin's mother, Nella, refuses to marry again.

Haus ohne Hüter shows that the victimization of postwar Germans by historical circumstances—the war and its aftereffects—is much more than that. It is a victimization by evil, by human wickedness and folly. Nella becomes a war widow because her husband, Rai, was deliberately sacrificed to the offended vanity of his wartime commanding officer, Lieutenant Gäseler. Rai,

Nella, and their child are victims, not of impersonal historical forces or social determinants, but of a villain's chicanery. Böll thus clearly presents a morally determined chain of cause and effect.

The unmasking of apparently social and economic causes as moral, psychic, and spiritual problems is essential to Böll's early novels. (In the later novels it is unnecessary, since the moral and spiritual basis of human behavior is explicitly shown from the beginning.) In *Und sagte* the marriage of the two persons through whose perspectives we experience early postwar Germany is apparently destroyed by the strains and stresses of overcrowded living conditions. On a deeper level, however, it is not the external situation that determines the fate of the marriage, but the husband's inner conflict between the drive for selfish freedom and the restrictive obligations that monogamous love and fatherhood impose. Self-indulgent *eros* and self-curtailing *agape* struggle in him for the possession of his soul. Essentially we witness not a social, but a Christian problem clothed in social and economic guise. The subtle interaction between the disguise and the underlying psychic and moral truth informs this novel with an inner tension that makes *Und sagte*, after *Wo warst du, Adam?*, Böll's artistically most successful work.

The conclusion of *Wo warst du, Adam?* (1951), the earliest of Böll's novels, takes place in the concluding stages of the Second World War. It can be taken as an apt point of departure for a closer consideration of the perspectives on postwar Germany given in Böll's three longest and latest novels, *Haus ohne Hüter, Billard um halbzehn* (1959), and *Ansichten eines Clowns* (1963).

At the end of *Wo warst du, Adam?* two perspectives converge upon a German town as the war is drawing to a close. The town lies in a no man's land between the American troops, who are not yet ready to enter, and the German army that, obedient to Hitler's command, refuses to give an inch. From the windows of the town's houses fly white flags of surrender.

One perspective is that of the German deserter Feinhals. The town is his home and he has decided that as far as he is concerned the war is over. Before descending, he gazes down upon his native place from an adjacent hill. Feinhals is a decent chap; he despises the Nazis and has always been defeatist about the war. He fell in love with a Jewish girl, Ilona (who, without his knowledge, has meanwhile been murdered in a concentration camp), and he looks forward to his homecoming and a modest career. Above all he plans to savor the joy of being alive.

The other perspective is that of the German army post located on another hill above the town. The post has orders to observe the town and bombard it in case of suspicious activity. There is "suspicious activity," since an American vehicle drives over from the American-occupied area and parks for a while in front of a certain house. The vehicle actually brings an American officer to his German sweetheart. The officer formerly in command of the observation post, knowing that the war was senseless and over in any case, but yet attempting to obey commands, spares the town and lets some shots fall in a swampy marsh nearby. Schniewind, however, new commander of the post, an ambitious and insecure careerist whose war decorations are of very recent date, resents the "traitorous" white flags and decides to punish the town. He shoots into it. One of the grenades kills Feinhals as he is about to enter his parental home.

This conclusion of Böll's war novel adumbrates his subsequent novels about postwar Germany in a number of ways. The opposition between Feinhals and Schniewind as representative characters of Germany anticipates the structural basis of the three novels: *Haus ohne Hüter, Billard um halbzehn,* and *Ansichten eines Clowns.* In these novels the descendants of Feinhals and Schniewind face each other as victims and victimizers both during and after the Nazi period. The Feinhals group of characters are decent, kind, and gentle. These characters are lovers of life, opponents of war, and haters of Nazism. Both during and after the Nazi era they are destined to be victims of the Schniewind type. The Schniewind characters are vain, ambitious careerists, profoundly insecure, and obsessed with the need to collect worldly honors—the craving for war decorations characterizes them. They are fanatics and bullies, petty, mean, and contemptible. Naturally, they are or were ardent supporters of Nazism and the war. Feinhals' descendants are simple, humble, and self-assured. Life and love are self-evident values for them. Schniewind's descendants are those who fear and hate life, twisted egotists in constant need of being reassured. The slightest opposition unnerves and infuriates them. In the display of love and friendship they see provocations to be punished. It is symptomatic and symbolic that the "suspicious activity" observed by the German post is a love tryst between two recent enemies, and that what particularly annoys Schniewind is the display of the white flags of peace.

Apart from the general dualism represented by the two camps (so reminiscent of Dostoevsky, whom Böll, in a recent interview,[1] named as one of the most important influences on his development), particular details of structure link Böll's novels of postwar Germany (the exception of *Und sagte* always understood) to the pattern established by the end of *Wo warst du, Adam?* In all three novels the bloodstained inheritance of Nazism and war overshadows the postwar period. In that past, Nazis or militaristic supporters of the war committed the direct or indirect murder of good, innocent persons. In each case the murderers are inferior, vain, narrow, pretentious, obviously insecure, and thus easily provoked to anger like Schniewind in *Wo warst du, Adam?* Their victims are infinitely superior to them. They are cut off in the flower of their youth, and because of their innocence and capacity for enjoying life and love their death appears all the more horribly and tragically senseless, a wasteful sacrifice without meaning, a destruction of human values never to be recouped.

In all these cases there is a surviving witness to the murders, as the orderly, Bechtels, in *Wo warst du, Adam?*, who witnesses Schniewind's decision to bombard the town. In the later novels this witness-figure is at the same time a victim who managed to survive. He was very close to the sacrificed victim—friend, comrade, or brother—and the same fate threatened him. He merely

[1] "Interview mit sich selbst: Heinrich Böll," *Die Welt der Literatur*, II, xxii (October 28, 1965), 13.

happened to be spared by a fluke or accident. His traumatic experience suffered in the Nazi period shapes the postwar life of the witness. He cannot and will not forget and forgive. The traumatic confrontation with violence and evil has doomed him for life and he cannot cease to suffer from his irredeemable loss. We are put in mind of the biblical meaning of "witness," as one whose life is dedicated to a truth he has seen. In postwar Germany, Böll's witness-figure lives in self-chosen seclusion and will have nothing to do with the accepted mores, fashions, and powers of the Bonn Republic. An inward petrifaction, an absence of all ambition and worldly interest, characterizes him. Most perspectives of Böll's novels are the perspectives of such shocked and hurt witness-figures, who carry the deep wound of what they saw into the postwar era. Such witnesses are Albert in *Haus ohne Hüter,* who had to watch his best friend being sent to death on the Russian front because of the vindictive petty spite of the fanatical careerist Gäseler and narrowly escaped his friend's fate; Robert Fähmel in *Billard,* who cannot recover from the knowledge that the finest youths in his city had been executed by the Nazis; his friend Schrella, surviving witness to the execution of his friends; Robert Fähmel's mother, who identified herself with the persecuted Jews and went to the railroad station to accompany them on their wretched journey to the death camps; the clown in Böll's last novel, who saw his older sister being forced by their fanatical Nazi mother to fight the "Jewish Yankees," as his mother calls the approaching Americans, and to die when the war was practically over, and who himself was almost shot as a defeatist the day the Americans arrived.

Other characters in Böll's novels are not actual witness-figures, but are otherwise close to the murdered victims. Prime example is Nella in *Haus ohne Hüter.* In a sense, she is also a witness, since she knows through Albert the circumstances of her husband's death and the name of the man responsible.

These witnesses and victims, surviving in postwar Germany, live curiously detached lives. They are so deeply hurt that they are not able to recover and overcome their traumatic loss. They have renounced all desire to participate in life. They keep, often outwardly and always inwardly, aloof from society and resemble relics from a bygone era. The tragedy of postwar Germany, as seen through Böll's perspectives, is this nonparticipation of her best children, who are too bruised to be of use. Nella, in *Haus ohne Hüter*, refuses to remarry and instead drifts in and out of meaningless affairs because she is resolved never again to offer the reassuring sight of a happy wife and mother to the country that murdered her husband. The appearance of domestic bliss would be an advertisement of forgiveness and forgetfulness to which she will not lend herself. The fact that murder could and did happen eliminates for her the possibility of a meaningful future. Although Albert, in contrast to Nella, takes an interest in the future generation, he, too, has been inwardly maimed. He has become an odd, solitary bachelor type—even though he had once been married—and has lost the artistic talent he once possessed. He literally lives off his past, maintaining his job by contributing the drawings he had made before the war. Hollowed and emptied as he is, he cannot hope to recover the inventiveness and verve that make the drawings of his youth a commercial success now.

Robert Fähmel, in *Billard um halbzehn*, leads a life of inhuman formality and rigid routine. To his young secretary, who cannot comprehend a life so lifeless and devoid of human spontaneity and warmth, he presents a disquieting enigma. He who has the talent to be a first-rate architect does not take up architecture after the war. He is content to serve as a humble consultant in statics. What he has witnessed under the Nazis has killed all creative ambition in him. His life now is only a shadow of what it might have been and a memory of the hurt received long ago. Like Nella, Robert Fähmel denies himself the act of re-creating. Nella will have no part in the re-creation of a happy family, and Robert Fähmel will not contribute his talent to the re-creation of the ruined German cities. Both choose frozen sterility and activities as near to utter meaninglessness as possible. Robert Fähmel shuts himself off from life in a minutely regulated and deadening routine. To avoid all human contact, he conducts his consulting services not by appointments, but only by correspondence. The daily ritual of his billiard game, to which he retires each morning at half past nine, symbolizes his withdrawal from life.

Schrella, in his London exile, has similarly withdrawn into the routine of teaching German grammar in an English school. He refuses to find renewed attachment to his native city, and to life itself, when he pays a visit to the scenes of his past. Remaining streets and buildings can no more bring back to him his murdered past than the middle-aged sister of his murdered comrade can take the place of that comrade himself. Like Nella and Fähmel, Schrella declines to make the gesture of reconciliation with normalcy, which, in his case, would be to return from exile. The remembrance of that which they witnessed remains the basic truth of these lives—a truth they will not change, cover up, and, least of all, forget.

An extreme form of exile from normal life is the insane asylum to which Robert Fähmel's mother was retired after she witnessed the deportation of the Jews and where she still finds herself sixteen years later. There cannot be a more telling detachment from the bustling and forgetful new normalcy of postwar Germany than life among the extreme deviants from normality. An equally unequivocal commitment to the perpetuation of protest is the unwillingness of the clown in *Ansichten eines Clowns* to conform to the expectations and the ambitions of his parents, acquaintances, and mistress, who want him to be more than a simple clown. In the end, he becomes that most embarrassing deviant in the society of the *Wirtschaftswunder*— a beggar. Protest and alienation cannot go further.

In *Wo warst du, Adam?* the life of the victimized witness to Hitler's war is snuffed out physically on the threshold of the postwar world. The lives of Böll's subsequent witness-figures are cut off emotionally, arrested and frozen inwardly, before they enter the postwar era. It is their destiny to be permanently estranged from the life of their country.

The complementary side of this victimization of the best is the continuing triumph of the worst. Nothing has basically changed since the Nazi period. The confrontation of anti-Nazi victim with Nazi victimizer persists in the postwar years in essentially the same constellation as during the Nazi era. The Nazis, now ex-Nazis in thin disguises, continue to rule; the anti-Nazis stay powerless, relegated to the periphery, as they had been before. In *Wo warst du, Adam?* Feinhals, the good man and anti-Nazi, is killed, while Schniewind, his Nazi killer, survives, dominating the field. It is symptomatic that Feinhals suffers his fate almost under the noses of the Americans. This spatial arrangement shows that the military victory of the Allies and the occupation of Germany will neither dislodge the Nazis from their positions of power in German society, nor aid and protect their victims. To be sure, the Nazis and the militarists will disguise themselves as democrats and may even believe in the form of government brought to them by their Anglo-American conquerors. Yet their inner nature will remain the same. They undergo no change of heart, but, at best, a change of ideology. In new costumes they retain their old personality and influence. In *Haus ohne Hüter* former Nazis, under old and new Christian labels, are the shapers of the cultural scene, and go on speaking of "elites." Lieutenant Gäseler, murderer of the anti-Nazi poet Rai, has made a splendid career in postwar Germany and becomes a powerful editor. In *Billard um halbzehn* Nettlinger, one-time right-hand man of the Nazi chief of police, holds semiministerial rank in the Bonn Republic and is a V.I.P. of the first order. Schrella, on the other hand, his former victim, finds himself again in a German prison because a Nazi warrant for his arrest is still in force in 1958.

There are ironic touches: In *Haus ohne Hüter* Gäseler plans to publish the poems of the man he murdered. In *Billard* Schrella owes his release from the prison of the Federal Republic to his one-time Nazi torturer, Nettlinger, which does not prove the ex-Nazi's kindness, but rather shows his power and influence in the Bonn Republic. To be sure, Nettlinger now sails under the flag of democracy and seems to believe in it quite sincerely. Yet, like all the former Nazis in Böll's novels, he proves inwardly unchanged, and his new convictions are, therefore, utterly

superficial. What made him a Nazi originally—the need to re-
assure his ego by impressing and browbeating others—continues
to operate in him and to shape his behavior, as his bullying
treatment of an old hotel porter shows; and, as proof that
political attitudes depend on moral and psychic factors, Böll
shows Nettlinger having difficulties resisting his urge to join
his old Nazi comrades as they assemble for their first postwar
parade. Similarly, ex-Lieutenant Gäseler, who pretends that
he wishes to forget the war, cherishes the first-name basis of his
relationship to Rommel. In postwar Germany these former Nazis
and militarists have remained in positions of command even
though they are unrepentant and unregenerate human beings.
Their victims, on the other hand, insofar as they have survived
at all, remain as isolated, peripheral, and impotent as they had
been under Nazism. Covered by a thin veneer, the old Nazi state
of affairs persists; the former distribution of power prevails.

This pessimistic view derives from the essentially Christian
dualism underlying the structure of Böll's novels. In them, the
anti-Nazis resemble the persecuted and despised followers of
the Lord, martyrs and confessors of the truth. A small band
of the forlorn few, they face the huge army of the wicked,
who rule the world for Satan. Nazi Germany had waged the
ancient war of evil against innocence with brutal frankness.
Postwar Germany continues it subtly and hypocritically.

The opposition of the two camps reaches, in Böll's novels,
far beyond Nazism and anti-Nazism. It is ultimately not a political, but a moral, spiritual, and religious dualism, which is
founded on Christianity but has a Manichaean element in it. The
Nazis' persecution of their victims is seen as a variant of the
age-old battle between good and evil, light and darkness, holy
grace and unholy power. The specifically Christian note of this
dualism is the presentation of the good as persecuted and op-
pressed, while the evil flourish in worldly success and prosperity. On one side we find the small flock of God's elect, his
chosen people and "lambs," on the other side the prospering
crowd of the wicked, favored by fortune and rich in worldly

honors, but devoid of all grace and inner contentment. Nazism is only an extreme manifestation of eternal evil.

Böll's dualism receives its most explicit, allegorical formulation in *Billard um halbzehn*. In this novel Germany (and mankind) is divided into two groups: One group consists of those who have consumed the sacrament of the buffalo, which is the sacrament of violence, and they form the vast majority. The other group, a tiny minority, consists of those who follow the sacrament of the lamb of peace. The latter refuse to partake of the sacrament of violence and are, therefore, destined to be the victims of violence. They will, in each generation, be singled out for persecution by the followers of the buffalo. Nazism is a phase in the buffalo's timeless orgy of oppression. In the 1930's the Nazi bully Nettlinger led the other boys in terrorizing Schrella, who was of the lamb's brotherhood. In the 1950's the bellboy Hugo suffers the same kind of juvenile persecution, but now no Nazis are among the tormentors. Hugo, gifted with marvelous charm and grace, is by his very grace and gentleness fated to be in his generation what Schrella was in the last—the lamb that forever arouses the buffalo's urge to persecute and violate. We are reminded of Abel, who, favored with the grace of the Lord, aroused the murderous envy of Cain. The symbolism of lamb and shepherd used by Böll establishes immediate associations not only with Abel, the shepherd slain like a lamb, but also with Christ, who is lamb and shepherd, sacrifice and judge, in one. As we shall see, in Böll the lamb sometimes becomes shepherd; the victim may turn judge. In that ancient battle between buffalo and lamb, Cain and Abel, world and Christ, labels and watchwords change, but the essence remains the same. In this struggle the lambs, who are not of this world, must go under, while the buffalo wins and reinherits, again and again, the power and glory of this world. In the framework of Böll's dualism, the Nazi type, therefore, cannot be truly defeated, but after each apparent defeat continues to hold power and victimize the good.

As stated before, Böll produces the image of Germany

through perspectives, through literal as well as figurative views. The physical or mental act of viewing a place, a scene, a person, has decisive structural and symbolic significance in Böll's works. The world of his novels is a focal area of converging perspectives. The perspectives of Feinhals and Schniewind, each viewing the same town from differing hills, prefigures the interplay of perspectives in Böll's later novels. Feinhals' home town obviously represents Germany situated between peace and war, Americans and Nazis, hope for survival and desire for destruction. Literally as well as symbolically it is a focal point of two converging but hostile perspectives.

The act of seeing is structurally and symbolically decisive at the end of *Und sagte*. Having separated from his wife, the husband sees a woman in the street who moves and fascinates him with a strange intensity. Tense with excitement, he watches the stranger, follows her with his glances, and discovers that she is his wife. Seeing through the perspective of estrangement teaches him that the woman who touches his life's nerve, the woman destined for him, is his wife. He sees her now as if for the first time, and this view restores in him the sacredness of his marriage, against which he had rebelled. From a distractedness of the heart, which used poverty as a pretext, he had degraded marriage to the imitation of an illicit love affair conducted in hotel rooms. The visionary recognition of his wife shows him the sacrament as his inner truth. The husband's last words, "nach Hause" (homewards), with which the novel closes, point to a spiritual significance contained in the physical homecoming to wife and children.

The importance of view and vision in Böll's work becomes clear to us when we recall the thematic and structural significance of the witness-figure. A witness, we must remember, is one who sees and on the basis of his vision testifies to the truth. Böll's novels are told from the point of view of victims and witnesses. The view of victim and witness tends to become, in his later novels, the view of accuser and judge.

The view of the avenging judge forms the nucleus around which *Billard um halbzehn* is structured. Robert Fähmel executes Hitler's scorched-earth strategy literally with a vengeance. Ostensibly an instrument of the buffalo, he avenges the martyred lamb. He becomes a demolition expert in order to blow up prized buildings and monuments of his buffalo-worshipping nation. In the enemy's service, he explodes the enemy's pride.

Robert Fähmel's judgment on the objects of German national pride—monuments and precious buildings—is literally based upon the act of viewing. Perspective and action merge in this novel. Taking the view of the object and determining the *Schußfeld* is the condition for executing the moral judgment and verdict of condemnation. The accusing witness and judge's view carries the plot both literally and figuratively.

With each act of viewing Robert Fähmel delivers a judgment. As he gazes out on the lobby of the fashionable Hotel Prinz Heinrich his vision transforms the hotel guests into damned souls in hell; his look pronounces the Last Judgment. His billiard game serves as the opportunity to review, in his mind's eye, the persecutions he witnessed and the vengeance he devised. Contemplating his past, he, at the same time, spreads it out before the curious gaze of Hugo the bellboy, one of the lambs of the next generation. From his secluded hotel suite Robert Fähmel looks out over the roofs and spires of his native city of Cologne and regrets that his work of vengeance has spared so much. "St. Severin," he remarks with self-reproach, "has escaped us." [2]

For Robert's father, Heinrich Fähmel, the act of viewing is likewise judgment and condemnation of the thing viewed. As he looks out over the familiar skyline of his city—its war-damaged silhouette intact again—he combines the external view with the inner review of his life, and judges it an aberration.

In *Haus ohne Hüter* we view Rai's murderer, Gäseler, through the witness, Albert, who relates the murder, and through Rai's widow, Nella, who is eager to avenge her husband. These two viewings of Gäseler form two bridge posts, as it were—one in the recollected past, the other in the im-

[2] Heinrich Böll, *Billard um halbzehn* (Cologne & Berlin: Kiepenheuer & Witsch, 1959), p. 250. ". . . am Horizont die Beute, die uns entgehen sollte: St. Severin."

mediate present—that connect two major strands of the plot like
a bridge across time. Planning her revenge, Nella literally views
Gäseler, as she sits next to him in his car. The man she sees
now, however, is too trivial to serve as the objective of something so great and meaningful as vengeance.

A similar shift in the would-be avenger's intentions occurs in
Billard, again as the result of a physical view of the target of
revenge. Released from prison, Schrella gazes at Nettlinger, his
one-time persecutor and torturer, and the executioner of his
friends. Schrella realizes that the long-hated enemy is only a
small, ludicrous figure. Nettlinger's presence proves physically
nauseating, but fails to arouse the slightest feeling of hatred in
Schrella. Likewise, Robert Fähmel's mother yearned for an opportunity to kill those Nazi officials of her city who were responsible for so much suffering. Yet when the occasion does
come and she views, with loaded pistol, the former Nazis pre-
paring for their parade, she sees them as a group of aging, pathet-
ic, and ridiculous philistines—museum pieces not worth a bullet.

These insights into the futility of vengeance, which occur
near the end of Böll's novels, are never signs of Christian forgiveness. Böll, with his nearly Manichaean separation of good
and evil characters, never presents contrition and regenera-
tion in the villains, nor do his characters refrain from retribution
because they feel that judgment belongs to God alone. They re-
nounce vengeance because the final view of their antagonists
gives them an understanding of Nazi evil that is akin to Hannah
Arendt's view of it in *Eichmann in Jerusalem*.[3] The Nazi villains
turn out to be banal philistines and petty snobs who lack all
access to the daemonic. They are merely bores, and boredom
makes vengeance irrelevant. These Nazi murderers are not in
the least diabolical. They are small and laughable men who do
not have the slightest inkling of the scope and the meaning of
their actions. Lieutenant Gäseler not only is unable to recall
that he had met the man whom he had sent to death; he cannot
even remember with certainty that he had ever been at that

[3] Hannah Arendt, *Eichmann in Jerusalem: A Report on the Banality of Evil*
(New York: Viking Press, 1963).

front sector. The deed that for others snuffed out all meaning
life had held has left no imprint on his mind. Such a man is
too deficient in spirit to savor the evil he has caused; and it is
only such conscious savoring by the villain that makes sense of
revenge.

In Böll's novels, however, a sharp distinction is made between
vengeance on individuals and the struggle against Nazism or,
more broadly speaking, the attitudes of which Nazism formed
the most vicious manifestation. Viewing the personal enemy
makes vengeance seem fatuous; viewing the scene of the enemy's
actions or the works of his pride confirms the resolve to battle
against him.

In *Haus ohne Hüter* Albert lets the boy Martin view the
underground prison where the Storm Troopers tortured Martin's
father and slew his Jewish friend, Absalom Billig. Showing him
the locality, he enjoins Martin to remember all his life that it
was the Nazis who had beaten his father and killed his father's
friend, that these horrors were real, once, that they had actually
and truly happened at the place where Martin now stands.
Looking at that spot and hearing Albert's words, Martin keenly
feels the reality of the evil that had existed. His recognition
of it counteracts and overcomes the effects of his teachers'
attempts to whitewash Nazi guilt. At school he had learned
that the Nazis were "nicht so schlimm" (not so bad).[4] The
concrete view of the scene of their activity brings him nearer
to the cruel truth, and ensures that the fight against the evil
that was Nazism will continue in the next generation.

Robert Fähmel, as we have seen, dedicates his whole life to
vengeance; but it is not a vengeance against individuals. He
punishes human pride by leveling its objects. In Böll the deadly
sin of pride appears in its specific modern form as snobbery.
It is the bread of the unholy sacrament of violence. Snobbery
invests the architectural monuments and landmarks of one's
country with an aura of national superiority. Snobbery ranges
in Böll from gluttonous ostentation to arrogant intellectualism.

[4] Heinrich Böll, *Haus ohne Hüter* (Cologne & Berlin: Kiepenheuer & Witsch,
1954), p. 284.

In all its varieties, however, it contains two principles: hierarchy and exclusiveness. The soldier's mania for collecting war medals and decorations—a *leitmotiv* in the stories and novels of Böll; the officer's insistence on having his rank respected and obeyed; the Nazi's racial arrogance; the gourmand's gorging himself while others have to starve; the gourmet's connoisseurship; the clique member's contempt of the uninitiated; and the intellectual's sneer at those educated in other ways than himself: all these are the variants of snobbery in Böll's work.

In Böll's perspectives snobbery always embraces cruelty. There is cruelty in the gloating emphasis with which Martin's grandmother, in *Haus ohne Hüter*, seated in an expensive restaurant, tears apart and devours her portion of lamb. She and all other diners in that plush restaurant consume their food as though proclaiming their triumphant power in the universe. The view of this frightens the boy Martin and sickens him, just as Schrella, in *Billard*, becomes sick watching the meticulous expertise with which Nettlinger chooses and consumes a meal. Martin finds no relief until his stomach yields up the food he has reluctantly taken in. The refusal of Martin's body to become part of the orgy of stuffing oneself—so characteristic of German life in the initial stages of the *Wirtschaftswunder*—adumbrates, subtly and symbolically, the theme that *Billard* states with allegorical explicitness. Martin identifies with the lamb and, therefore, cannot eat it. Like the followers of the sacrament of the lamb in the later novel, Martin excludes himself from the sacrament of violence into which his anxiety-inspired vision transforms the restaurant. These bourgeois diners seem to be performing a cannibalistic ritual. Viewed by the outside, they have become a savage society which bestows status upon those who can kill, lacerate, and consume the greatest number of victims. The novel makes an implicit connection between the smug voracity of these gourmands and the murderous cruelty by which the Nazis realized their idea of social exclusiveness and superiority. In Böll the ultimate form of snobbery is murder. Murder drives exclusiveness, on which all snobbery is founded, to its logical conclusion.

A subtle form of snobbery is found to be the decisive flaw in Heinrich Fähmel's life, as he reviews it. He had possessed grace. He was talented, worked without effort, was distinguished by suppleness of body and mind. Frail of build, a spiritual type, he resembled a young rabbi. Heinrich Fähmel's Jewish appearance confirmed the impression that he was one of the chosen. For in Böll's works Jews are always among the elect, endowed with grace, but victimized and slain by the envious descendants of Cain. The racially Jewish girl, Ilona, in *Wo warst du, Adam?*, whose marvelous singing in the extermination camp affirms the Creator in the midst of hell, and Absalom Billig, in *Haus ohne Hüter*, whose brilliant caricatures of the Nazis earned him their special hatred and destined him to be the first Jewish victim in his city, both exemplify the role of the Jews as vanguard in the ranks of Abel. With his frail Jewish looks, Heinrich Fähmel was marked as one of the victim- and witness-figures and consequently won the love of his saintly wife.

Heinrich Fähmel, however, had strayed from his nature. He compromised with the world. He betrayed himself by adopting the appearance of snobbery, which is the mark of Cain, the sign of the buffalo's sacrament. Heinrich Fähmel's snobbery was based upon his decision to get on in the world and adapt himself outwardly to the violent buffalo. His motives were basically the same as those of Martin's grandmother in *Haus ohne Hüter*, as she gorged herself in the restaurant to prove to herself how distant she now was from the wretched poverty of her childhood. Heinrich Fähmel, too, was desperately resolved to escape the grinding poverty of his youth once and for all, and to succeed in a world in which snobbish self-esteem creates the aura needed for success. Taking his daily breakfast in the Café Kroner bestowed that aura of distinction upon Heinrich Fähmel. The Café Kroner routine symbolized his surrender to the world. It was alien and opposed to life with his wife at home. (She never accompanied him to the Café.) Heinrich Fähmel attempted to live in both worlds. His heart remained with the lambs; but his façade was established among the worshippers of the buffalo. He was ready to serve the powers that were and gave his share to his country's war effort. The formula worked. He succeeded famously among the respectable and violent. The first, and most gratifying, token of his success was his victory in the competition for building the new abbey of St. Anton's. He obtained the order to build it, and the abbey became one of those architectural landmarks of which educated Germans were proud.

The conflict, however, between his true nature, represented by his marriage and home life, and his social role, symbolized by the Café Kroner, was reflected in the radically opposed characters of his sons. Otto, adopting his father's outward adjustment as his own inner conviction, became a Nazi; faithful to his father's original nature, Robert joined the persecuted lambs as their "shepherd" and helper, and lived to annul his father's work.

In the end, Heinrich Fähmel comes, independently of Robert's judgment, to the same conclusion. Because it had been divided between personal truth and public falsehood, he judges his life as wanting, and condemns the public façade and the monument it has become as worth being defaced and spat upon. When he learns that it was his own son who had blown up the monument of his fame, the abbey of St. Anton's, he approves with relief. What his son had destroyed was a false idol, a monument to his and his country's disastrous egotism. As he brings his wife home from the insane asylum to which he had allowed the Nazis to consign her, he discontinues his breakfast ritual at the Café Kroner. His last act in the novel is to repeat symbolically the execution of his pride which his son had performed actually; he cuts into the birthday cake which had been presented to him in the shape of his famous abbey and joyfully proceeds to demolish it.

The Catholic author Böll chooses a Catholic monument to represent false values. Destroying his father's abbey, Robert Fähmel executes judgment over the self-betrayal of Catholicism. This is, indeed, a major theme of Böll's more recent novels. A significant shift in the role played by Catholicism, and Christianity in general, occurs in his work.

In the early *Wo warst du, Adam?* Catholicism plays an entirely positive role. It shames and inwardly overcomes the concentration camp commander. His victim, distinguished by grace, is Jewish by race but Catholic by faith, a combination that infuriates him. Upon his command, she sings Catholic hymns with an artless perfection that proclaims the grace within her and testifies to God and life eternal. The message reaches him as it refutes him, his ideology, and his whole way of life. Killing her and ordering all Jews massacred immediately, he admits his defeat and confirms her victory; for his rash action thwarts all his plans and shows that he has lost all control of himself. He has his pet project and possession, his choir of Jewish inmates, wiped out with the rest of the camp. That strange choir, art literally imprisoned, had served the gratification of the commander's snobbery. As owner of such an oddity in an extermination camp, he appeared as a connoisseur, a capricious and refined Nazi, one possessing the power to indulge strange whims. Issuing forth from the voice of the Jewish girl, Catholicism proves its triumph by driving him to destroy the object of his special pride.

Und sagte also presents Catholicism positively. The husband's final recognition of his monogamous love, his wish to return to his family and home, are consonant with the Catholic view of the sacredness and the sacramental character of marriage. Organized Christianity begins to play a negative role in *Haus ohne Hüter*. Although most of the good characters are churchgoing and genuinely pious, the villains in the novel are militant Christians. The leader of their circle, Schurbigel, attempted to infuse Christianity into Nazism and advocated joining the Storm Troopers in order to Christianize them from within. Here we come upon one reason why Christianity is connected with negative characters. These "Christians" opt for compromise with worldly ambition. They wish to join the violence of the world with one half of themselves, while keeping the other in the camp of Christ. Thereby they commit the kind of self-betrayal by which Heinrich Fähmel jeopardizes his grace.

The guilt of the militant Christians in *Haus ohne Hüter*, how-

ever, is even more fundamental. After the war and the defeat
of Nazism, they use the prestige of Christian views to re-
habilitate themselves and rise to dominant positions in the postwar world. They make of Christian culture and politics the
fashionable cult of a clique, to which they can tie their careers.
They sin against the Christian spirit of humility and nondiscrim-
ination. Although calling themselves Christians, they exercise
the arrogant exclusiveness that was the essence of Nazism.

In this novel one may even detect a subtle parable of the
relationship between fallible churchmen and Christ. The poet
Rai, bearer of true grace, is slain. Afterwards he is idolized by
the churchlike coterie of intellectuals that is of one spirit with
the force that slew him. Indeed, his murderer has become a part
of the group. They abuse his name by exploiting it for the
reputation it gets them. Promoting the poetry of an anti-Nazi,
they can prove how anti-Nazi they themselves had been, whereas
it was they—one of theirs—who slew him.

St. Anton's abbey in *Billard* explicitly shows the self-betrayal
of the Catholics, that is, the betrayal of the lambs to the buffalo.
The monks of St. Anton's honored Hitler with torchlight
parades. This most obvious surrender to evil formed part of the
greater surrender to the spirit of nationalist snobbery which
weighed on St. Anton from its beginnings, since it was conceived
and built as a prominent cultural adornment, a stylish contribution to German cultural prestige. A church that caters to modish
aestheticism and vanity deserves to be leveled.

The role of Catholicism in *Billard* is the reverse of what it was
in Böll's earlier work. What we see of it now is not even ambiguous, as Christianity was in *Haus ohne Hüter*; it is entirely negative. In *Billard* Catholicism is clearly allied with the buffalo
and condones the persecution of the lambs, in whom we must see
symbolic representatives of the true Church. Yet even though the
perspective and the plot of *Billard* do mete out severe judgment
on the representatives of the Catholic Church, Catholics are as
yet merely subsidiary fellow travelers of evil, and not its prime
embodiment. In Böll's latest novel, *Ansichten eines Clowns*, however, militant and proselytizing spokesmen of intellectual Cathol-

icism are the primary antagonists and persecutors of the hero-narrator of the novel. Catholicism has suffered a complete reversal of its original function in Böll's work; it has become the villain.

The only positive character in *Ansichten eines Clowns*, the clown-narrator himself, is an agnostic. But he, the nonbeliever, is a good man, while the proselytizing Catholics, his opponents, are hypocrites and snobs. In the Germany of 1960 they are what the Nazis had been fifteen years before. In the Bonn of 1960 the clown suffers at the hands of the Catholics the fate that his older sister had suffered at the hands of the Nazis in the Bonn of 1945. The Nazis, above all the narrator's fanatical mother, had sent his sister to the front, to die a senseless sacrifice in a war already lost. Fifteen years later a circle of militant Catholic intellectuals proceed to kill her brother, in a less direct, more hypocritical way. These intellectuals convert Marie, the clown's love, to militant Catholicism in order to estrange her from him. Without her love, however, he cannot perform, and he becomes a cripple. The wound on his knee, which he received from a fall during his last ignominious performance, is more than physical. It symbolizes the mutilation of his faculties as an artist and as a man. Losing his beloved, he loses not only his happiness, but his livelihood as well. He can no longer hope to be the excellent clown he had been while he had her love as his support.

The clown's Nazi mother and the Catholic intellectuals of postwar Germany represent and enact the same attitude. In the name of an ideology, they destroy human life. Their ideological dedication is the means by which they are able to exercise their power and indulge their hostility toward the innocent, natural joy of life. The clown's mother is not only a Nazi fanatic, but an avaricious Spartan as well. She kept her children on a lean and joyless diet, and from principle denied them everything that might brighten and cheer their lives. Similarly, Böll's Catholics despise the unpretentious joy afforded by the clown's natural art, and resent the simple happiness of his relationship with Marie. Because they cannot bear the sight of such ingenuous and pure fulfillment, they are set upon destroying it. Cain's envy of Abel's grace remains for Böll, in this latest work, the archetypal model of persecution and murder, as it was in his previous works. From *Wo warst du, Adam?* to *Ansichten eines Clowns*, it is always the victim's grace that provokes the persecutor's vicious attack. Ilona's grace manifests itself in the effortless command of her voice, which makes of her song a perfect vessel of praise and joy, and it is this that enrages the concentration camp commander and makes him lose his self-control. Rai's and Absalom Billig's grace shines forth in the effortless flow of their creations, and, in Rai's case, the ease with which he wins Nella's heart. This provokes the vengeance of the scorned Hitler Youth leader and leads to Rai's torture in the underground stronghold of the SA. It is Rai's carefree insouciance, born of his grace, that infuriates Lieutenant Gäseler and impels him to have Rai killed. Hugo's grace makes him the favorite in his hotel, but also the butt of persecution by his schoolmates. Robert Fähmel is the champion of the high-school ball games where Nettlinger's envy turns into hatred. The grace of the clown shows itself in his perfect command of his body and the astonishing speed with which he had won Marie and turned her away from a Catholic youth leader. The Catholic circle cannot forgive the clown until revenge is accomplished and he is crushed.

The clown's father demands that the clown repudiate his particular art, which is his nature, and conform to his father's idea of what constitutes art. The father's view derives from the advice of a fashionable critic, an "expert," in whose judgment clowning is too ordinary and popular to be true "art." The clown can only become respectable by learning to be a mime. The son's natural, God-given skill is not good enough for his father. The latter, infected by the snobbery of the age, expects art to be a status symbol and conform to the hierarchy of snob values.

A wealthy businessman and television personality, the clown's father represents the world—big business, publicity, and naked economic power, gilded by circumscribed and recognized "culture." The Catholic intellectuals collaborate and unite with the world in destroying the clown. The father demands that the clown, by surrendering his art, betray himself. The Catholics demanded that he forget his love for Marie, which amounts to a parallel self-betrayal.

It is the irony of this novel that the agnostic clown is, in a fundamental sense, more truly Catholic than the Catholic ideologues who despise him. For he, the infidel, holds the Catholic idea of the indissolubility of marriage, whereas they not only persuade his wife to desert him, but also ask him to acquiesce to her new marriage to another man. As in *Und sagte*, monogamous love is, this time explicitly, the symbol of true Catholic Christianity. It is a token and a representation of eternity in earthly life. The clown's relationship to Marie is not consecrated by the Church; officially it is not a marriage. However, in the clown's heart his love for Marie is his marriage to her and there cannot ever be any other woman for him. His physical and emotional union with her has the force of a sacrament. Böll seems to adopt the view of his clown in *Brief an einen jungen Katholiken*, where he says: "It is impossible for me to despise that which is erroneously called physical love; such love is the substance of a sacrament, and I pay to it the reverence that I give to unconsecrated bread because it is the substance of a sacrament." [5] In deserting the clown and marrying one of the Catholic leaders, Marie transgresses against the Catholic idea, as interpreted by Böll. Canonical law, by sanctioning Marie's new marriage, contradicts the law of the heart. It consecrates a union that is betrayal of an existing love and therefore, according to the law of the heart, adultery. With this juxtaposition of religious essence and ritualistic legalism, of the true faith of the individual soul and the meretricious formality of the Church, Böll's clown approaches a position that is almost Protestant and is certainly romantic. The clown's position constitutes the extreme point of a development noticeable in Böll's work from its beginnings.

Böll cites the Protestant Kleist as his earliest and most profound literary experience.[6] There is indeed something of Kleist's ideal of the marionette-figure, an ultimately romantic and Rous-

[5] Heinrich Böll, *Hierzulande: Aufsätze zur Zeit* (Munich: Deutscher Taschenbuch Verlag, 1963), p. 29. [Passage translated by Professor Sokel—Ed.]
[6] See note 1.

seauistic ideal, in Böll's heroes—especially in those who, like Ilona, Rai, Absalom Billig, Robert Fähmel, and the clown, are artists or have something artistic in them. They resemble the marionette-type characters of Kleist—Alkmene, the Marquise of O——, Käthchen, and Michael Kohlhaas (Robert Fähmel, the implacable avenger, bears a profound resemblance to the latter). Like these Kleist characters, they possess the unshakable self-assurance and inner certainty that is the mark of innocence. As in Kleist, the primary conflict in Böll's work is that between innocence and worldly crookedness, between the purity of the simple, natural soul and the envious arrogance of the twisted careerist. But, whereas in Kleist innocence and justice win the battle in the end and force the world to acknowledge them, the contemporary author makes a distinction between the obvious physical victory that goes to the wicked and false, and an intangible, ill-definable, spiritual or moral victory that the just obtain for themselves.

Even in *Ansichten eines Clowns*—in a way, Böll's most pessimistic novel—a kind of victory is wrested from bleak defeat. For the clown is able to resist, and will continue to judge and to accuse. He will not be unfaithful to the memory of his sister's senseless sacrifice and he will not forgive her Nazi murderers; he refuses to betray the sacrament of love; and he will not surrender the art that is his nature. His triple loyalty makes him the figure who remembers in a world that wants only to forget. It also makes him a beggar, because the world will not support so uncomfortable a reminder. It is precisely as a beggar, however, that the clown fulfills his role, which is to be the fool in the traditional sense of the term—the jesting conscience of his society, the living contradiction of its pretended wisdom, the living refutation of its pretended happiness. At this point, I think, the perspective of Böll's character becomes the perspective of the author. Böll, who wrote the satire *Doktor Murkes gesammeltes Schweigen*,[7] considers his role in contemporary Germany to be not unlike the role of his clown. The clown's favorite

---

[7] Heinrich Böll, *Doktor Murkes gesammeltes Schweigen, und andere Satiren* (Cologne & Berlin: Kiepenheuer & Witsch, 1958).

game is "Mensch ärgere dich nicht" (Parcheesi), a simple, un-pretentious pastime, far below the intellectual prestige bestowed upon chess or the social prestige of bridge. It is this game Böll loves to play with his children.

Heimito von Doderer's *Demons* and the Modern Kakanian Novel

BY HEINZ POLITZER

University of California, Berkeley

My title may require a word of explanation. "Kakania" is derived from "K. and K.," *Kaiserlich und Königlich*, "Imperial and Royal," the official designation of the Habsburg monarchy. Robert Musil introduced the name "Kakania" in his monumental novel fragment, *Der Mann ohne Eigenschaften*, of 1930, and since then, especially since the end of the Second World War, "Kakania" has come to be synonymous with Austrian civilization, deeply rooted as it is in the spirit of the Baroque age and encompassing the regions under the sway of the Habsburg scepter—Austria and Hungary as well as the successor states which emerged after the collapse of the empire in 1918.

Kakania is an imaginary area, a realm of memories rather than a geopolitical reality. Its boundaries are fluid, its inhabitants figures of fiction. The name was coined and the concept established only after the Habsburg empire had ceased to exist, and yet Kakania has survived, as only a dream or a work of art can endure. The recent revival which the arch-Kakanian writer Franz Kafka experienced behind the Iron Curtain is an indication of the extension of Kakania's boundaries. Kafka is read and discussed in Prague and Warsaw, Budapest and Zagreb; he is even appreciated as far down the Danube basin as Romania, but he remains an unwelcome foreigner in East Berlin or Leningrad. That is, Kakania still lingers on where coffee is sipped in the comparative leisure of a coffeehouse and where literature is considered a necessary balance to the exigencies of politics. It evokes no existing country but a way of life, lost, to be sure, but still sought after as an inexhaustible wellspring of recollections.

In Musil, Kakania had formed the backdrop of a highly intellectualized comedy, performed with the detachment of rare and rarefied irony. Yet Musil had coined his term well. It connotes not only the comfortable glory of the Habsburg reg-

imen but also the Greek word *kakós,* which stands for bad or
evil and all sorts of unsavory associations. For Old Austria was
no heaven of fried chicken, no *Backhendelparadies.* Though it
still is popularly remembered as a stage where plays of elegance
and remorseless abandon were performed, its reality was colored
by doubt and despair. Not only did its inhabitants indulge in
easygoing dreams, they also were haunted by melancholy, doubt,
and despair. Franz Grillparzer's profoundly masochistic sarcasm
and Johann Nestroy's wit, which cut through society as if it
were a cake of mud, speak of the fact that all was not well in
the state of Kakania. The ingrained pessimism which imbued
Austrian literature from the fairy-tale world of Ferdinand Raimund—a suicide—to Arthur Schnitzler's moral skepticism reveals
an irritated uneasiness with the civilization to which they con-
tributed so much. Franz Kafka's nightmares are at least as
Kakanian as Franz Lehár's operettas. Psychoanalysis, with its insistence on the destructive compulsions and the fatal drives in
man's nature, is, after all, a thoroughly Kakanian product. So are
the revealing portraits of Egon Schiele and the younger Oskar
Kokoschka, as well as the tormented music of Arnold Schönberg, Alban Berg, and Anton von Webern—all of which have
spread Kakania's fame throughout the world.

As a frontispiece to his tragic report on the First World War,
Die letzten Tage der Menschheit, Karl Kraus chose the photo-
graph of an executioner, smilingly displaying the work of his
hands, the corpse of a hanged man, surrounded by equally
amused bystanders. Kraus used to call this portrait, that reeked
of the horrors of martial law and of the cruelty of those in
authority, "das österreichische Antlitz" (the face of Austria).
It was the portrait of Kakania. Conversely, Musil included
among figures which form the entourage of the "Mann ohne
Eigenschaften" (the man without qualities, or nondescript man)
the person of Moosbrugger, a convicted murderer and a denizen
of the lower depths of humanity. Moosbrugger, too, is a representative of Kakania. Musil was conscious of the sinister implications of the name he had ingeniously created as a highly ambiguous epithet.

It was precisely his intimate knowledge of the underworld which predestined Heimito von Doderer to become the chronicler of Kakania in its entirety. Born, in 1896,* into a distinguished and well-to-do Austrian family, Doderer has thoroughly experienced, nevertheless, the *kakós* in Kakania. He participated in the First World War, spending the years from 1916 to 1920 in Russia, first as a prisoner of war, then in a workshop, and finally on a trek home through the Kirghiz Steppe. In 1933 he joined the then illegal National Socialist Party of Austria but left it after the rape of his homeland in 1938. In 1940 he was converted to Catholicism, as a sign of protest, but also, as his *Diaries* show, from inner necessity. In the Second World War he saw service with the German Army, first in France and then again in Russia, until he was taken prisioner in 1945. Yet it cannot have been the disasters of war alone that exposed the writer to the demonic side of human existence.

Doderer's approach to the *kakós* in Kakania is not an intellectual adventure as was Musil's. It is based on an affinity which is perhaps less elective than the gentle reader would wish it to be. From the outset, he was possessed by a fascination with the eccentrics, and lived as a bohemian on the fringes of society. His understanding of the social outcast, the revolutionary, the prostitute, and the murderer is congenital. To a degree seldom experienced in the annals of literature he speaks their language, knows their habits, and is conversant with their sensitivities, as if he were one of their ilk. This asocial orientation of his thoughts and manners he himself once called "atavistic" when he compared it with that of his genteel origins.[1]

On the other hand, Doderer is an accomplished man of letters and a well-trained historian. His books abound with literary innuendoes and parodies. His *Die Strudlhofstiege* of 1951, which established him as a major novelist, is among other things, a

---

[1] *Der Spiegel*, June 5, 1957; quoted from Dietrich Weber, *Heimito von Doderer: Studien zu seinem Romanwerk* (Munich: Beck, 1963), p. 295. I am indebted to Mr. Weber for many an insight into the complex texture of Doderer's works.

*[Heimito von Doderer died after this article was set in type.—Ed.]

daring experiment in the treatment of epical space and time. *Die Dämonen* of 1956, with which we shall be primarily concerned here, takes its title from Dostoevsky, whose *The Possessed* is generally known in German as *Die Dämonen*. Both Doderer's *Dämonen* and Dostoevsky's *Possessed* are political novels about the madness inherent in politics; both are centered on ingroups, the Nihilists in the Russian, "Our Crowd"—a motley gang of middle-class Viennese—in the Austrian novel; both are climaxed by the catastrophe of a fire. The chronicler of Doderer's novel has a name, Geyrenhoff, with the same initial and final letters as that of Dostoevsky's narrator, Anton Lavrentjevitch G——ff; Geyrenhoff's name is, as often or not, abbreviated to "G——ff." In his *Diaries* Doderer refers to the Russian novel as a basic pattern which he has used as a substructure, not unlike the use James Joyce made of the *Odyssey* as a basis of composition for *Ulysses*. Moreover, *Die Dämonen* includes a chapter, "Dort unten" ("Down There"), describing, in fictitious fifteenth-century German, a witch-hunt privately undertaken by a Carinthian nobelman, Achaz von Neudegg. This chapter echoes the title of Joris Karl Huysmans' novel *Là-bas;* even its plot is vaguely reminiscent of the older writer's story about the fifteenth-century kidnapper Gille de Railles. An astonishing literary pastiche, this chapter also emulates Thomas Mann's exercises in late medieval German, which render parts of his *Doktor Faustus* so difficult to read. If the modern novel is characterized by the revival of older originals and by experimentation in the very material it consists of—language—then Doderer has quite consciously written an epic piece keeping abreast of the most recent exploits in his craft.

In short, Doderer is as much a sophisticate as one familiar with the primitive sphere of the social underworld. In his aesthetic writings and in his *Diaries* he is apt to explore the crisis of the modern novel and to make aphoristic observations on time, life, and the arts; at the same time he speaks the jargon, thinks in the idiom, feels with the nerves of the depraved and the disgraced, the possessed and the dispossessed, the scum, the *Ruaß* or soot covering the social fabric. Still more, in a kind of democracy of the demonic, he evens out the difference that seems to prevail superficially between the level of the under-world and the middle classes, from which most of his figures are taken. The result is a unity of approach to the world he has set out to depict.

Let me begin by giving an example. From a toilet window the prostitute, Anny Gräven, watches Meisgeier, the murderer, climbing up the wall of a house where he will kill one of her colleagues and friends. It is going to be an act of sheer terror, committed without apparent rhyme or reason:

> ... she looked up at the open window of the cubicle and then with-out a sound climbed up on the seat. At that moment Meisgeier's legs passed close by her nose; he seemed to be walking on the window cornice outside. Only a light scraping sound could be heard. He was making his way along the outside wall. Then she could see his whole body. He was outstretched along the opposite side of the air shaft, at about the height of the first story. And now he began moving silently upward between the dark windows. His long arms reached over his head; his slight body was drawn up with light and almost graceful movements. It all looked sure and effortless, The spectacle took Anny's breath away. It was an altogether in-credible demonstration of strength, skill, and courage . . .[2]

"It all looked sure and effortless." The first observation which forces itself upon the reader is the author's interest in the tech-nical aspects of the cat-burglar's display, and the obvious plea-sure he takes in describing it appreciatively. Technical skill of whatever kind is, indeed, one of Doderer's preoccupations. Of his own craft he would say, "The artist . . . works with his eyes cast down, watching his hands and all things technical." [3] In his attention to factual detail and in its smooth execution, meisgeier, the absurd murderer of *Die Dämonen*, resembles an artist, becomes an artist in his field. His skill ennobles him, though he threatens society like a huge polyp (the comparison

---

[2] Heimito von Doderer, *The Demons*, trans. Richard and Clara Winston (New York: Knopf, 1961), p. 609 [hereafter quoted as *D*].

[3] Heimito von Doderer, *Tangenten: Tagebuch eines Schriftstellers 1940–1950* (Munich: Biederstein Verlag, 1964), Preface [hereafter quoted as *T*].

is Doderer's). He is a master of his métier, just as the writer
is of his. This is what I have called the democracy of the demonic.

Who reports this scene? The German original of *Die Dämonen* bears the subtitle, "According to the chronicle of *Sektionsrat*
Geyrenhoff." Georg von Geyrenhoff, a prematurely retired civil
servant, is the main narrator as well as one of the principal
figures in the book. But neither he nor any of his informants,
among whom are two self-professed writers, Kajetan von Schlaggendorff and the historian René von Stangeler, serves as a
witness here; we see what we see through the eyes of the prostitute Anny Gräven but learn what we learn through the words
of the writer, who happens to be a connoisseur as highly ap-
preciative of cat-burglary and murder as of grammar and style.
In a passage like this, Doderer's attraction to the underworld
expresses itself in the language of the excellent writer he also
is. Only thus could Doderer hope to achieve what he frequently
calls a "total novel." To be sure, he is not content with weaving
the different strands of Viennese society into one coherent texture, he combines the conscious and the unconscious areas in the
psychological make-up of his personages in such a way as to
produce the universality of all things human. Nothing human
or subhuman remains untouched by him, and the limits of consciousness are boldly left behind to attain the representation of a
totality of description. To achieve this end, Doderer stresses
the facts and disdains the lyricism of subliminal associations as
much as the speculation of the merely intellectual.

The "total novel" is Doderer's answer to the crisis of the
novel which has marked German—and European—literature
ever since the turn of the century. It is perhaps worth remembering that a Kakanian, Hugo von Hofmannsthal, was among
the first to formulate this crisis as symptomatized by a breakdown of communication, in his letter of Lord Chandos, published in 1902:

... I have lost completely the ability to think or speak of anything
coherently. . . . The abstract term of which the tongue must avail

itself as a matter of course in order to voice a judgment—these terms crumbled in my mouth like moldy fungi. . . . The language in which I might be able not only to write but to think is neither Latin nor English, neither Italian nor Spanish, but a language none of whose words is known to me, a language in which inanimate things speak to me and wherein I may one day have to justify myself before an unknown judge . . .[4]

Although to some extent disguised by its mystical ending, this statement articulates the crisis of the word, which is by implication also a crisis of value and value-judgment. Doderer was to maintain much later that the crisis of the novel "would exist today even if there were no novel at all. It is a crisis of our reality in general, and the idea which has been questioned by it . . . is the idea of universality." [5] To overcome this crisis means to establish a new totality, and, since Doderer is first and foremost a novelist, he directs his efforts toward arriving at this new totality in the sphere of fiction. Here he seems to follow the example of the great Austrian novelist Hermann Broch, whose *Der Tod des Vergil* could be claimed to surpass even Joyce's *Finnegans Wake* in the search for universality.[6] As early as 1935, while celebrating Joyce's fiftieth birthday, Broch stated:

. . . the classical novel was satisfied with the observation of real and psychological life conditions; it was satisfied with describing these circumstances by way of the language. One simply acceded to the claim of viewing a slice of life through a temperament. One represented and used language as a ready-made instrument. What Joyce does, is infinitely more complicated. He is always accompanied by the insight that the object [of the narration] must not simply be put into the spotlight of observation in order to be described. Also the subject to be represented, that is, the "narrator as idea"

---

4 Hugo von Hofmannsthal, *Selected Prose,* trans. Mary Hottinger and Tania and James Stern. Bollingen Series XXXIII (New York: Pantheon Books, a Division of Random House, Inc., 1952), pp. 133–134, 140–141.

5 Heimito von Doderer, *Grundlagen und Funktion des Romans* (Nuremberg: Glock & Lutz [1959]), p. 35. [Passage translated by Politzer.—Ed.]

6 George Steiner, "The Brown Danube," *The Reporter,* October 12, 1961, p. 58.

as well as the language which he uses to describe the object of representation, are media of representation and belong to the act of representation. What he tries to achieve is the unity of the object and the means of representation in the broadest sense, a unity which certainly is sometimes apt to give the impression as if language were to overwhelm the object and, vice versa, the object were to overwhelm the language to the point of complete dissolution. However, this unity remains, avoiding any superfluous expletive, any redundant epithet; it remains a unity in which the one naturally grows out of the other, because it is in its entirety subject to the architecture of the whole.[7]

From this some insights can be gained into Doderer's technique. If it was not the chronicler Geyrenhoff who told the Meisgeier episode referred to before, can we not assume that it was Broch-Joyce's "narrator as idea" who told the event with undiminished satisfaction? In order to produce a "total novel" the narrator has to be omnipresent, perhaps disembodied into the "spirit of narration," as Thomas Mann calls him in *Der Erwählte*.[8] Though Doderer may claim to be a realist, or even a naturalist, the ubiquity of his "narrator as idea" puts his fiction on a consciously chosen suprareal level.

The ubiquity of the narrator imposes upon him one duty: he has to plan his novel as if it were based on an architectural grand design. Doderer has been observed to plan the structure of his novels on a drawing board.[9] *Die Dämonen* has been compared by one critic to a "rococo comedy crenelated with neo-Gothic," [10] by another, less well-meaning one, with "one of those vast government buildings erected by the Austro-Hungarian Empire and still in present use; it is monumental, but

[7] Hermann Broch, "James Joyce und die Gegenwart," *Gesammelte Werke* (Zurich: Rhein, 1952–1957) VI, 197–198 = *Essays, I. Dichten und Erkennen.* All rights reserved by Suhrkamp Verlag, Frankfort. [Passage translated by Politzer.—Ed.]

[8] Thomas Mann, *Gesammelte Werke* (Frankfort: Fischer, 1960), VII, 10.

[9] Herbert Eisenreich, "Biedermeier-Dämonen," *Reaktionen: Essays zur Literatur* (Gütersloh: Mohn, 1964), p. 130.

[10] H. M. Waidson, "Heimito von Doderer's Demons," *German Life and Letters*, New Series, IX (1958), 218.

parts of it seem vacant and have a musty air." [11] Although, as
we shall see, fragmentation of plot and atomization of suspense
belong among Doderer's techniques, there inevitably is in his
work a ground plan, which, however, reveals itself in all its
architectural mastery only on second or third reading. Like
most modern fiction of the highest order, Doderer's novels
open themselves only to the devotee prepared to cooperate with
the author and to work seriously with the text he is reading. His
novels are less *romans fleuves* than *romans mosaïques*. Since *Die
Dämonen* is also a mystery story, the seemingly arbitrary re-
fraction of plot contributes greatly to the suspense and its resolution.

As far as plot is concerned, Robert Musil declared flatly in his
Mann ohne Eigenschaften: "The plot of this novel results in not
telling the story which was supposed to be told." [12] Doderer is
more cautious:

I have reached the point [he said in 1940] where I realize that a
novel cannot be written at all according to a "theme"; it can only
originate from a figure or figures or from a basic narrative idea, however technical, since such an idea contains the figures in its very in-
ception. But the narrator must not under any circumstances recognize a theme which is carried out by his figures because, by doing
so, he would absolutize his theme and elevate it beyond the real
level which consists in the fact that the narrator exists only in the
psychology of his figures. There can be no theme except as it is
imagined by individual figures in the novel; another existence is not
becoming for a theme, least of all [the role as] a principle which
guides the author. The author can only imagine persons, not ideas.
People must not be understood as ideas which have become concrete,
as it seems to be the case in the drama, but all [can] only [be
grasped] as psychological partial spheres of the figures whose existence reaches in many a way far beyond them and which are controlled also by quite different mechanisms and, for all this, in a
decisive way.[18]

11 Steiner, "The Brown Danube," pp. 58–60.
12 Robert Musil, "Aus einem Notizbuch (1932)," *Der Mann ohne Eigenschaften* (Hamburg: Rowohlt, 1952), p. 1640.
18 *T*, p. 38. [Passage translated by Politzer.–Ed.]

Doderer seems to set novel against drama when he relegates the sphere of ideas to a part of the figures he describes, namely, the consciousness of their deliberations and actions. For him ideas are silently understood; in the drama they are expressed and take shape in the figures which recite them. The unconscious as well as the vast twilight area on the threshold between conscious and unconscious remains inaccessible to them and must therefore not be explored by the novelist. (This distinguishes Doderer's work from the "psychological" novel of Proust and Mann, Broch and Joyce, and relates him, to a certain degree, to the psychological vacuum existing in Kafka's novels.) He is not even primarily interested in psychology. The novelist, he was once heard to say, ought to use psychology only as an expedient; in actual fact the epic writer is not a psychologist but a "fatologist," [14] that is, not a diviner in the vast land of the human soul but an interpreter of fate in its innumerable interactions with man's psyche. This, too, is part and parcel of the totality he attempts to reach in his books: he does not explore the unconscious but embodies it in the changes and happenings it brings about. To be sure, for Doderer, fate is not the inexorably frozen mask of a Greek god, it is a truly Kakanian mixture of half-smile and half-tear, embodied in the bitterly humorous career of action and dialogue which his figures perform, and is, above all, revealed by the ambiguous cadence of a word rather than by the thunderbolt of life.

More profoundly, however, Doderer's resistance against ideas does not stem just from his antipathy against the drama. (He has written distinguished poetry and is an accomplished critic but has kept himself aloof from the stage.) Like most Kakanian novelists since the turn of the century, Doderer is more concerned with the wisdom of the well-turned phrase than with an overall philosophical structure for his writings. His forte is the aphorism and the repartee, and not the intellectual message of his books as a whole. This distinguishes Kakanian novelwriting from that farther north, in Germany. "The Germans

[14] Herbert Eisenreich, "Heimito von Doderer: Die Vereinbarkeit des Unvereinbaren," *Reaktionen*, p. 200.

save themselves with their intellect," he has the scholar Scolander, say in *Die Dämonen:*

... while the Austrians do the same with their vital juices. Each has his own way. Only the future will demonstrate who comes out better in this test: that is to say, who retains more of his humanity. In both cases the sources of error are inordinate, for only both forms of reaction taken together could really be called intelligence . . .[15]

Generalizations of this sort are, of course, more a pastime than a source of insight. Nevertheless, they have been indulged in, and by Kakanian writers with a special relish. (Remember, for instance, Hofmannsthal's paradigm, "Prussian and Austrian," of 1917![16]) Yet there is a piece of sound self-criticism in Scolander's remark. Doderer's books are not written with the help of his intelligence as, say, the books of Ernst Jünger are; they originate indeed in his "vital juices" and stem, as the German original has it, "aus den Geweben" (from his tissues). Thus, the substance of Doderer's writing is the rank flesh of life itself, breathing under the luxuriant skin of his style. His intelligence neither adds to the organic growth of the body of his narratives, nor does it press the abundance of fact and detail into the patterns of an overall philosophical design. The technical mind of the author simply watches that, once constructed, the outline of his plan is not overgrown by excrescences of his naturally sprawling language.

As mentioned before, the insistence on beautiful language seems to be one of the characteristics of Kakanian literature. Quite apart from the magic of Hofmannsthal's language (he wrote, however, only one novel, *Andreas*—and this novel remained a fragment), it is worth remembering that perhaps the best narrative prose in German was written during our century by Joseph Roth, a Galician Jew turned Catholic and Monarchist. Roth's *Radetzkymarsch* has long since become a classic, if only among the happy few. And although Musil and Broch are

15 *D*, p. 1150.
16 Hugo von Hofmannsthal, "Preusse und Österreicher: Ein Schema," *Prosa* (Frankfort: Fischer, 1952), III, 407–409.

certainly more intellectual than Doderer, they, too, glorify, in the final analysis, not the thought but the word. Both the grandeur and the weakness of the Kakanian novel lie in its native fascination with the power of language. Kakanians are born, though often frustrated, lyrical poets. Take, for instance, the prose poem that concludes Broch's *Der Tod des Vergil*. This passage performs the feat of representing the very act of dying, the gradual transition from life to death, of Virgil. It is an apotheosis of the word, which occurs in the end as it was in the beginning. This prose poem consists of one overlong sentence and represents what it describes: the ultimate victory of language over life *and* death:

The rumbling continued and it was emitted from the mingling of the light with the darkness, both of them roused by the incipient tone which now actually began to sound, and that which sounded was more than song, more than the striking of the lyre, more than any tone, more than any voice, since it was all of these together and at once, bursting out of the nothing as well as out of the universe, breaking forth as a communication beyond every understanding, breaking forth as a significance above every comprehension, breaking forth as the pure word which it was, exalted above all understanding and significance whatsoever, consummating and initiating, mighty and commanding, fear-inspiring and protecting, gracious and thundering, the word of discrimination, the word of the pledge, the pure word; so it roared thither, roaring over and past him, swelling on and becoming stronger and stronger, becoming so overpowering that nothing could withstand it, the universe disappearing before the word, dissolved and acquitted in the word while still being contained and preserved in it, destroyed and recreated forever, because nothing had been lost, nothing could be lost, because end was joined to beginning, being born and giving birth again and again; the word hovered over the universe, over the nothing, floating beyond the expressible as well as the inexpressible, and he, caught under and amidst the roaring, he floated on with the word, although the more he was enveloped by it, the more he penetrated into the flooding sound and was penetrated by it, the more unattainable, the greater, the graver and more elusive became the word, a floating sea, a floating fire, sea-heavy, sea-light, notwithstanding it was still the word: he could not hold fast to it; incomprehensible and unutterable for him: it was the word beyond speech.[17]

". . . the word of discrimination, the word of the pledge, the pure word . . . the word [hovering] over the universe . . . the word beyond speech"—this is the creed of many a Kakanian writer. Broch, who once took issue with Hofmannsthal in a brilliant, long essay, nevertheless proceeds here from the pained insights of the Chandos letter, developing them in the direction of the linguistic mysticism of Ludwig Wittgenstein and *his* "word beyond speech." The word as lodestar of life and literature, the word hidden in gesture and even silence: this is the Kakanian tradition in which Doderer stands and on the basis of which his work discloses itself most easily.

To be sure, there is a definitely Proustian ring in Doderer's aesthetic program, which he uttered, significantly enough, in French: "Écrire, c'est la révélation de la grammaire par un souvenir en choc" [18] ("Writing is the unveiling of grammar by the shock of remembrance"). But you have to note that this self-styled "naturalist" and "fatologist" does not set out to reveal reality but grammar (though this grammar may well be the syntax of human life) and, by doing so, still harks back to the word worship of his predecessors. The emphasis he puts on remembering as a creative act not only conjures up the image of Marcel Proust but also is reminiscent of a statement made by Harry Levin with regard to James Joyce's *Ulysses* and enthusiastically repeated by Thomas Mann as a summation of his *Doktor Faustus:* "The best writing of our contemporaries," Harry Levin says, "is not an act of creation, but an act of evocation, peculiarly saturated with reminiscences." [19] *Die Dämonen,* which was twenty-five years in the writing, is likewise told from the vantage point of reminiscence: the action takes

[17] Hermann Broch, *The Death of Virgil*, trans. Jean Starr Untermeyer (New York: Pantheon Books, 1945), pp. 481–482. Reprinted by permission of Pantheon Books, a Division of Random House, Inc.

[18] Doderer, *Grundlagen*, p. 27.

[19] Quoted from Thomas Mann, *Die Entstehung des Doktor Faustus* (Stockholm: Suhrkamp, 1949), p. 83.

place in 1927 but is told in 1955, twenty-eight years later. The
nature of this evocation Doderer has expounded in great detail
in his *Diaries*, published under the title, *Tangenten* ("Tangents"),
in 1964. [20]

Yet Doderer is not content with writing another novel in the
crisis or producing another "work in progress." Above all, he
is factual. Preservation of data seems to him the most urgent
task of the novelist. Although he is an accomplished historian—
he was made a member of the exclusive "Institute for Austrian
Historiography" in 1950—he is doubtful of the power invested in
his discipline to prevent historical fact from disappearing. "No
professor like Ranke, Niebuhr, or Mommsen will register the
essential features of our day," he wrote. "Instead, fiction will." [21]
To be sure, the modern novelist may, by his own choice, hide
the facts in his text like Easter eggs. Whereas Musil's plot exists
in its nonexistence, the action in Doderer's book is concealed
behind a multitude of plots, subplots, and superplots. Each of
these plots seems to have a center of its own. The difficulty
these episodes offer to the reader as well as the affinity they
seem to have to life consists in the fact that the individual
plot centers are not harmonized and often not even manifestly
related to one another. They occur at random within the grand
design of the novel. They form an anecdotal galaxy and often
blind the reader's eye instead of enlightening him. Yet this
diversity of seemingly incompatible episodes contributes to the
totality of the novel Doderer hopes to achieve. For this totality
is meant to evoke, on the level of language, the absurdity and
the glory of existence.

To narrate, then, means to unravel the texture of fate. "In
fact," Doderer says in the "Overture" to *Die Dämonen:*

. . . you need only draw a single thread at any point you choose
out of the fabric of life and the run will make a pathway across the

[20] "Epilog auf den Sektionsrat Geyrenhoff: Diversion aus 'Die Dämonen',"
T, pp. 51–100 *passim*.

[21] Heimito von Doderer, "Österreich: Bilder seiner Landschaft und Kultur,"
Orbis Terrarum: Österreich (Zurich: Atlantis, 1958), p. 5. [Passage translated
by Politzer.—Ed.]

whole, and down that wider pathway each of the other threads will become successively visible, one by one. For the whole is contained in the smallest segment of anyone's life-story; indeed, we may say that it is contained in every single moment; start up your dredging machine and you take it all up, no matter whether ecstasy, despair, boredom, or triumph happens to fill the moving buckets on their endless chain of ticking seconds.[22]

Here Doderer himself seems to compare his world to a whore's stocking, which the reader has to unravel, thread after thread. Time, again, is a vast dredging machine, sifting and ordering the primal substance of the world. This world of many segments, each seen in its own perspective and arranged around its own center, takes in the prince and the pauper, the bank and the brothel, game and revolt, children's joy and innocence lost, meeting and alienation, gossip and wisdom, aesthetic reflection and demonic destruction, fire and ice, and the unfathomable absurdity of existence. Or, to put it more simply, these books will survive, if for no other reason, because they register the inventory of a civilization in its totality. They will live on because they consist of grammar, that is, the order of language which conquers the fun and the mess of life.

Die Dämonen is a very long novel, 1,329 pages in the English translation, followed by a publisher's list of characters numbering no less than 142 names, with 31 starred as main figures. Apart from this list, the reader is well advised to have a street map of Vienna at his elbow, for the movements of the figures across the boundaries of the city represent many important ups and downs in their social and human careers. When Leonhard Kakabsa, the workman-turned-librarian, crosses the bridge which leads from the proletarian suburb to the palatial center of the city, he not only moves from a near-slum to the core of an intellectual commonwealth, but also becomes at long last the man whom the "fatology" of his author had meant him to be all along. The crossing of the bridge stands symbolically for Leonhard's *Menschwerdung*, the fulfillment of his human destiny.

[22] *D*, p. 7.

Vienna, which Doderer has called the "chymical" melting pot of East and West, is at the same time described as a metropolitan village, a *Weltdorf*, the center of the author's universe. The parochialism for which Doderer has been widely criticized in this country turns out, however, to be a blessing in disguise. For the image of the city, which arises in the novel as an eternal and indestructible landmark, has prevented the narrative from drowning in a troubled sea of the tragicomic. However haunted by their demons these Viennese are—and not a single one remains untouched—there is the archetypal mother image of Vienna to balance their eccentricities and deviations.

The novel is climaxed by the burning, at the hands of an incensed and uncontrolled mob, of the Vienna Palace of Justice on July 15, 1927. Inasmuch as this event opened for the first time to its true dimensions the rift between the two major parties of Austria—the Social Democrats and the pseudo- and crypto-Fascists—it was a prelude which precluded any concerted political action on the part of Austria as a whole when Hitler invaded the country eleven years later. Thus the fire is meant to anticipate the fall of Austria and the holocaust of the Second World War. It also ended, in Doderer's opinion, whatever freedom Austria possessed after 1918, by allowing the mob to take over the regimen. Thus the destruction of an ugly and by no means architecturally impressive government building assumes a figurative meaning, almost comparable in importance with the storming of the Bastille, only in reverse order: here liberty was gained, there freedom was lost.

In the burning of the Palace of Justice the demons which have lingered "down there" in the slums of the city as well as in the unconscious of its inhabitants appear in broad daylight. It is a veritable Witches' Sabbath. The absurd reigns supreme. The police fire at people who are close to them in their social origins. They die at the hands of workmen. Leonhard Kakabsa and two of his old friends bend over the corpse of a policeman who was Leonhard's friend. The image of Justice is enveloped by flames. An old woman lies in her blood, which mingles with the milk pouring from a jug in her hand; the red and the white form the colors of the city of Vienna. Humanity crumbles to a heap of nonsense, like a jigsaw puzzle under the fist of a mischievous child. With a complicated instrument Meisgeier fells the police from a sewer where he hides until he is shot and falls back into the waste water. The soot, the *Ruaß*, tarnishes the countenance of the city and compromises the cause of the socialists. Young boys overthrow the pole of an arc lamp. And all this bedlam forms a superb piece of writing with which there is little to compare in the Kakanian letters of this century.

Yet the destruction is not seen only with the eyes of the chronicler, the *Sektionsrat*, whom the author has cleverly posted in a building next to the scene of the action. It is viewed also from above, from the heights of the Vienna Forest, the Cobenzl Hill, and from this elevated observation point the demonic outburst finally falls into place. The conflagration appears like a "red pimple" on the face of the city.[23] But pimples are a minor and transitory distortion. The upheaval is minimized when it is viewed in the context of the city, which for Doderer is the eternal one. Here, as elsewhere, Vienna forms the second focal point of the novel, the first one being, of course, the Demons themselves.

Vienna is for Doderer what Paris was for Balzac and Jules Romains, Dublin for Joyce, or Prague for Kafka's *Der Prozeß*: an almost mystical point of orientation. "Never does a major city cease to exist within one and the same span of human memory *(Äon)*," Doderer says in his essay on Austria: "it does not stop existing even if it is completely destroyed, and this in a quite material sense." [24] Thus Doderer sees Vienna outlive the catastrophe of July 15, 1927, as well as the other more formidable ones the city suffered at the end of the Second World War. And indeed, the city has been resurrected. As far as *Die Dämonen* is concerned, the image of Vienna not only forms the counterpoint to the innumerable individual voices conjured up in the course of the novel but also remains a constant, untouched and indestructible, a "first reality" which

23 *D*, p. 1276.
24 Doderer, "Österreich," pp. 12, 14.

lends sense and proportion to the "second reality" of the demonic aberrations of its inhabitants. It is more than its parts; it survives them in indisputable grandeur. In this glorification lies the "metaphysical dimension" of the novel.[25] It is easy to deride this idea as a characteristically Kakanian mystique, born of the wish-dreams of a small and defeated people. If it is a mystique, however, it is used very functionally, since it keeps the balance with the otherwise dissipated action.

Doderer is very fond of the designation, "second reality." It appears in his diaries as well as in *Die Dämonen* with ever increasing frequency. "Strolls in a second reality are never profitable," he will say. "And it is characteristic of all matters connected with the demonic that, although they create a tremendous stir and a great deal of motion, they never leave anyone with anything substantial in his hands afterwards." [26] From this utterance and similar ones it is easy to conclude that this "second reality" is more or less connected with the concept of the demonic proper. The "first reality" is the idea of a safe and sane world, of an imaginary Vienna, for instance, whose fame the novelist proclaims although the historian is fully aware of the demonic forces that have torn the face of the city in the past. Nevertheless, the "second reality" encroaches upon the first as a fantasy, as often as not as imaginings of sex and violence; its mark is a state out of focus and, finally, the inevitable decline. "Every achieved second reality must burst sooner or later," Doderer has one of his figures say.[27] It ends in utter disillusionment or what the writer calls at one point, "the fall from the hobbyhorse." [28] And yet—the "second reality" is almost exclusively the subject of *Die Dämonen* and requires for its representation the "total novel," whereas the "first reality" expresses itself in silence, by a fleeting memory, or the modesty of a simple gesture. It becomes artistically manifest primarily in its relation to the "second reality," such as the city of Vienna, which emerges as an eternal principle in relation to the demonology of its inhabitants.

[25] Weber, *Heimito von Doderer*, p. 229.
[26] *D*, p. 1024.   [27] *D*, p. 1057   [28] *D*, pp. 836 ff.

Die Dämonen is a book about this "second reality." Within
it reigns a continuous interchange, a sliding from episode
to episode, the very simultaneity of actions which seemingly fail
to be directed toward a common narrative center. It can be
argued that this principle of simultaneity, where one subplot
opens into another without logical transition, is deeply ingrained in the Kakanian character. One of Hofmannsthal's early
poems comes to mind:

> Doch ein Schatten fällt von jenen Leben
> In die anderen Leben hinüber,
> Und die leichten sind an die schweren
> Wie an Luft und Erde gebunden . . .
>
> Viele Geschicke weben neben dem meinen,
> Durcheinander spielt sie alle das Dasein . . .[29]

Within the sphere of Doderer's "second reality" there is a
constant change, an interrelatedness of the incompatible, a per-
petual opening of hands, ready to take rather than to give.
Shadows of alien existence envelop the individual until he becomes a shadow. The easygoing and the heavy embrace until
both have lost their specific weight. The subhuman touches the
human until humanity itself is put into doubt. The episodes turn
into agonies and subside as suddenly as they have appeared.
Outlines are blurred and the reader stumbles from event to
event, as if he were moving through a city of apparitions. The
very virtues of the "first reality" turn out to be the vices of the
"second." Take, for instance, Vienna itself. The open traffic be-

---

[29] Hugo von Hofmannsthal, *Gedichte und lyrische Dramen* (Stockholm:
Bermann-Fischer, 1946), p. 20.

> Yet from their existence falls a shadow
> Reaching the existence of the others,
> And the light ones are bound to the burdened
> As to earth and air . . .
>
> Many destinies are woven together with mine,
> Living plays them all through one another . . .

Adapted from the translation by Vernon Watkins in Hugo von Hofmannsthal,
Poems and Verse Plays, Bollingen Series XXXIII. 2 (New York: Pantheon
Books, a Division of Random House, Inc., 1961), p. 35.

tween East and West, left and right, low and high, of which the
city boasts, degenerates into fancy-free round dance performed
by the most disparate dancers. The drunken bouts of the ad-
venturers Eulenfeld and Körger; the embezzlement committed
by the Financial Counselor Levielle; Kajetan von Schlaggendorff's broken marriage and his near-incestuous relationship
with his presumed sister Quapp; but also the Fascist activities
of the Hungarian contingent; the threatening bankruptcy of one
of Austria's greatest banks, the Kreditanstalt; and—last but not
least—the tragedy of July 15, 1927: all these are symptoms of
a universal suspension of clear limits, of a deep-seated per-
missiveness and sloppiness of conduct. Here Doderer shows the
dirty reverse side of Kakania's shining currency. Nestroy had
chastised this sloppiness of Kakanian life, and Karl Kraus had
branded it, deploring the absence of clean and clear thought and
language. And Doderer? Precisely because he refrains from psy-
chologically motivating the actions and speeches of his figures,
these actions and speeches assume the air of aimless drifting.
There is considerable charm in this sloppiness of the soul, this
Seelenschlamperei, which extends to the areas of political maneu-
ver and financial speculation. Existence is dissolved into a play
with word and feeling; idiosyncrasies are derided and yet taken
seriously, like Schlaggendorff's "Memoir on the Fat Females" or
Jan Herzka's preoccupation with the tortures suffered by medieval witches. Everything touches on everything without penetrating it, and even the deepest wound leaves no scar. Comedy flourishes: the ease with which Quapp von Schlaggendorff slips from
the arms of her lover into the embraces of her bridegroom-to-be
is the stuff operettas are made of; it hardly weighs more
heavily than the meeting across all borders of probability
between genteel Mary K. and Leonhard Kakabsa, obviously
meant as a reward for the latter's *Menschwerdung*. Even the
most consistent part of the plot, the story of an embezzled last
will, is not solved in the decisive way of a true mystery story
but allowed to drag on toward its happy resolution under the
benign prodding of Geyrenhoff, the chronicler. In this novel
everything is possible and nothing necessary. *Tout comprendre*

est tout pardonner spreads its twilight over the "second reality." Half-deeds and half-wishes are symptoms of the disturbances visited upon the characters of the book. "I did not want it to happen," these words which Emperor Wilhelm the Second uttered after the outbreak of the First World War and which Karl Kraus has God Himself speak as an epilogue to his *Letzte Tage der Menschheit* are the unwritten motto of *Die Dämonen.*

Yet one would go astray if one were to consider Doderer a moralist trying to support the normalcy of a "first reality" in its struggle against the aberrations of the "second." He thinks too highly of the "first reality" to make it dependent on his support. What he writes is primarily a tragicomedy of demonic manners. He does not take sides, he abstains from preaching, and, in a way which is as gentle as it is unmistakable, he pokes fun at any preachment his chronicler or any other figure may deliver. For preachments derive from what Doderer calls a "pseudology." In his diary he says, "The wish to move where one can only be moved is the root of all sexual pseudology—the example or paradigm of all the many other pseudologies—and at the same time the basic mechanics of the total state which sets systematic aims to what is essentially aimless—a consolidated derailment." [30] Inasmuch as the burning of the Palace of Justice is a forerunner of the total state of Nazi dictatorship, it is the visible climax of the many pseudologies with which *Die Dämonen* abounds. Sexual pseudologies complement the political ones, as often as not even in the same figure. Thus, Captain von Eulenfeld, the leader of an unruly gang, the *troupeau*, is shown both as a Fascist and as a philanderer; while Imre von Gyurkicz, Quapp's first lover, is killed in front of the Palace of Justice, haranguing against the police, seemingly on the side of the workers, in truth, however, because he, too, has succumbed to his human and political pseudology. To unmask these pseudologies as pseudologies would result in a new pseudology. Quite in general Doderer fails to indicate what his figures should do or avoid. "This is the way we look," he seems to be saying—add-

[30] *T*, p. 642.

ing, perhaps, in an undertone: "Not a very pretty picture, is it?"[31]

The cadence of Doderer's style is the unhurried one of a raconteur's ramble. This is the attraction as well as the danger of his method as a narrator. Bearing the overall plan in mind, he tells his books rather than composes them. The living memory of his city, remembering a thousand anecdotes, *aperçus*, witticisms, and actual happenings, Doderer abounds with tales, small and tall. The simultaneity he practices in his total novel is the outward expression of this abundance. Moreover, he is a wise man, and since he is afraid of succumbing to pseudologies, he hides his insights in asides and carefully tucks them away where they are least expected. Thus one chances upon a passage like the following:

As we grow older the summers seem shorter; winters form the measure of time, with only intervals between them. These summer intervals are often terrifying; they seem to surround the heart with a padded silence. The selfsame summer which in youth seemed endless now assails us with a mute pressure, so that we feel we must stop and grab at something, grasp something. But what is there to hold on to? Where can the hand find support?[32]

This could be the melancholy reflection of a Biedermeier writer clad in the images of modern isolation; in any case it is an ageless testimony to the enduring message of life and decay, of the ebb and tide of the seasons, the seasons of the year as well as of man's existence proper. Asides like this provide the novel with surprising vistas at practically every turn; yet they are not, as in Musil, the structure upon which the "essayistic" narrative rests. Much rather they are small insignia woven into the texture of the tale. When they occur, the narrator simply interrupts and reflects for a while before he takes up his tale again.

Where, finally, is Doderer's place in Kakanian literature? Is he an end or a beginning? Does he fit into the tradition and wait for disciples or does he crown the structure of Austrian literature in the manner of a solitary keystone?

The tone and the scope of Doderer's novels are thoroughly his own. In a literature dedicated to the preservation of the beautifully *written* phrase he has introduced the relaxed cadence of the appropriately *spoken* word. The inflection of Austrian speech, the dialect which is spread equally across all the strata of Viennese society, survive in the *Sprechton* of his books. His telling them rather than writing them gives these novels an archaic quality. Here, at long last, is a narrator of epics in the time-hallowed sense of the old tellers of tales. In this respect, he is the crafty bard of the saga of Kakania.

Personally, I very much doubt that Doderer will pass on to his juniors the natural cadence of style. Among the younger writers it is Herbert Eisenreich who seems most fascinated with Doderer's tonal complexity. He has tried to emulate the older writer, apart from having written several enlightening essays about him. But Eisenreich is much more of an eclectic and intellectual than Doderer; the sovereign and comprehensive view is missing from his short stories.[33] He is nervous, where Doderer is maliciously benign; pugnacious, where the senior man is ironic; a figure in the game which his master is playing.

On the other hand, Doderer has acquired a place among those writers who try to lead the modern novel out of its present crisis. He is an experimenter, especially given to the exploration of the element of all narrative: epical time. Yet, although he embarks on experimentation more often than not, he also includes traditional forms taken from the novel of manners, the mystery story, even the educational novel (as evidenced by Leonhard Kakabsa's development). Thus he is able to establish a certain balance between the new and the old. His novels are conclusive: "I do not write fragments," he said,[34] with an unmistakable stab at Robert Musil, whose example seems to bewilder him most. The veritable rash of marriages which breaks

---

[33] For example, *Schöne, wilde Welt* (1957), *Der Urgroßvater* (1964), and *Sozusagen Liebesgeschichten* (1965).

[34] Weber, *Heimito von Doderer*, p. 291, n. 91.

out at the end of *Die Dämonen* has even reminded one critic of the old adage, "Bella gerant alii, tu, felix Austria, nube" ("Let the others wage war, you, happy Austria, marry").[35] Marriages, however, are a comedy device derived from the Spanish stage and practiced, for instance, by Nestroy as a conventional favor to his audience to conclude even his most acid satires. In a similar spirit Doderer denies himself the "open ending" by which the modern novel seems to lead into infinity but ends, as often as not, in bitter uncertainty.

He does not look for undue depth, and has found, as did Hofmannsthal, the profundity of existence on its surface. What distinguishes *Die Dämonen* from the "trans-real" fiction of our time is its preoccupation with human fact and detail. By incorporating fact into fiction, Doderer catches the very totality of the "first" and "second realities." Reading his books, you learn about Kakania, the gloriously corrupt country, and its society. You meet its people, and people in general. Doderer seems to address whomever he tells about. (This, too, is a characteristic of the novel of manners.) This gives to his books a definite popular slant. But, like all the great regional novels, *Die Dämonen* is meant to transgress the boundaries of its locale. In its combination of the demonic and the eternal, of the existential and the popular lies Doderer's contribution to the European novel of the future. Non-Kakanians are just as welcome to it as are Kakanians.

[35] *Ibid.*, p. 178.

The Present Quandary of
German Novelists

BY GERD GAISER

Pädagogische Hochschule, Reutlingen

I must preface this essay with a modest disclaimer: Not being a literary historian or critic, I am unaccustomed to weighing the pros and cons of a matter objectively, or to outlining and analyzing a development. Nor am I a systematic, indefatigable reader, always thoroughly informed about the latest events on the literary scene. Moreover, as an author I do not represent any particular literary movement or group. It would perhaps not be irrelevant to mention that my own writing career began comparatively late in my life. I started out as a painter, and my present occupation[1] brings me into daily contact with the plastic arts and artists, not with literary circles. Therefore I entreat the reader to understand the following reflections as those of a private individual—not one standing above the melee and drawing general conclusions about it, but one caught in the midst of the fray, a combatant, with a necessarily limited and subjective viewpoint.

My purpose here is to provide insight into a contemporary novelist's difficult situation. In some respects the things I describe will be generally applicable to all novelists, in other respects they will be peculiarly German, in still others, merely personal. Let us suppose that an author either has just begun writing a new novel, or has paused before his task is completed. This author is no longer a neophyte; he has outgrown that happy first stage when the creative impulse is pure and strong, when the creatures of one's imagination seem to be real living beings whose actions are almost independent, to be watched almost with curiosity. No longer is this the case! The author is now assailed by doubts: What has he gotten himself into? How is he going to achieve his purpose? What means are at his disposal? What would other authors do? Most disturbing of all, he can-

[1] [Since 1962 Dr. Gaiser has been a professor of art at the Pädagogische Hochschule in Reutlingen.—Translator.]

not evade the one essential question: What really is the nature of his task? Is it a genuine service, the thought of which can justify his work and support his morale while he is performing it?

It may sound excessively solemn to speak of the *mission* of literary works. I shall not shrink from using the term, however, nor from applying it specifically to an art form, the novel. For it is a foregone conclusion that literature in the broad sense, that is, everything communicable and every type of communication, has a mission.

In the Western humanistic tradition it is accepted practice to speak of the detachment that characterizes a genuine work of art. Art is supposed to be free of any suspicion of ulterior purpose; it is essentially *play*, pure and sublime play. The work of art is a phenomenon whose origin requires no explanation; it serves no person and no cause, and is justified by its own perfection. Without taking aim, it nevertheless hits the mark, and in a great variety of ways. The effects it produces on people can be unpredictable, and its rich texture constantly invites new interpretations. In the course of time opinions change and different aspects of the work are highlighted.

I submit that this established notion about art may no longer be valid in this technical age of ours. We are beginning to perceive that literature has a remarkably tough, durable consistency; that is to say, its character as art is not necessarily dissolved when an element of purpose is added. In the realm of scientific illustration the reproduction of a plant, a human face, or a landscape, primarily intended for documentation and information, can sometimes achieve the rank of art. The same is true in scientific writing: A report, a treatise, a notice can attain the level of literary art, and still retain its purpose intact. Indeed, the purpose is served more efficiently because of the artistic excellence. The German language has a special term, *Kunstprosa*, for nonfictional works of art. The writer of *Kunstprosa* does not have to fret about the question "Why am I writing? What goals am I pursuing?"

The novelist is not so fortunate. Some, to be sure (and I am not just speaking of hacks), can confidently state, "I wrote this novel to proclaim the injurious effects of alcoholism, and that one to warn against the careless handling of money." On the other hand, there is the case of the author (of my acquaintance) who, when asked, "I presume you are treating the problems of community housing in this novel?" answered, after a pause, "You may be right, but I am not ábsolutely sure." It would be unwise to dismiss his answer as careless and irrational. Like the question itself, the author's reply is an indication that some serious and even profitable consideration was given to the problems mentioned—and an indication of something else: André Gide, never accused of being a confused thinker, once encouraged his readers to explain his books to *him*, instead of the other way round, because, as he said, "There is always *more* in them." [2] The novelist does not set out to frame a treatise, a polemical text, or a proclamation; his intention is to create a novel. But aspects of these other things may incorporate themselves into his text. The novel is fiction; it is, to use a German word that has unfortunately lost some of its former luster, *Dichtung*. It arises from an *artistic* impulse. We may be able to isolate this impulse and to examine it from various sides, but we cannot explain it; it simply has to be accepted as a human phenomenon: Man is a being who demands art and is able to produce it. This is not to say that we are prevented from investigating the *function* of art. The epochs dominated by magic and credulity had their own concept of the function; for us, however, the matter must be viewed in its social context.

Let us now return to our hypothetical author: What is his relationship to the reader? How does he view the reader? Does he make concessions to him? Does he await instructions from him? Obviously there are some novelists who study the market

[2] See André Gide, *Paludes,* 72nd ed. (Paris: Gallimard, 1951), preface, p. 11: "Avant d'expliquer aux autres mon livre, j'attends que d'autres me l'expliquent. Vouloir l'expliquer d'abord c'est en restreindre aussitôt le sens; car si nous savons ce que nous voulions dire, nous ne savons pas si ne ne disions que cela.—On dit toujours plus que CELA. . . . Attendons de partout la révélation des choses; du public, la révélation de nos œuvres."

and attempt to supply what the public wants, more or less subtly, depending on their ability. But the novelist to whom the work itself is more important than its potential salability faces a more complex situation. Does he so much as have the reader in mind as he writes? I believe he cannot help doing so. He may not think of the public in general; he may communicate spiritually with a single imaginary reader. And even if he does without this imaginary reader, the very fact that he is working with *language* involves him inescapably in the process of communication. Language, that great anonymous creation, is not the property of the author alone. All his future readers have a share in it and are themselves busily occupied in shaping the constant alterations of the linguistic substance. In this sense, they are co-authors with him. Thus there ensues an exchange, a give and take. And one other productive role is assigned to the readers: If they are true readers, then they do for the literary work, as it were, what the player does for a musical composition—they perform it.

Accordingly, the author summons his reader; to what extent this summons is a challenge will be discussed later. "Gentle reader" was the charming formula used in older novels (and when I was a child these words always evoked a very concrete image of an amiable countenance bent over an open book). What can the contents provide, what will they provide? In spite of the much-heralded "crisis" of the novel, in spite of the widespread doubts whether storytelling is of any significance, whether it is fungible, or even possible anymore, the reader can still derive naive pleasure from feeling empathy, from following the course of events, from being diverted. If narrative art is experiencing a crisis, then certainly it is not one of the readers' making. Even intellectually demanding persons who want more than a mere plot cannot fail to be pleased when a story is *well* told. Good storytelling is a hard task for the writer, especially if he is more inclined to reflection than to observation. In Germany so-called popular novels are sharply distinguished from real, or serious novels; it would be thought almost a disgrace if the latter read well, or were exciting. Recently, however, a born storyteller has appeared on the scene in the person of the novelist Grass (to mention only one example). The force of his talent for telling stories has swept aside our doubts about the survival of storytelling in our age. Declare the novel dead or not, the experience engendered between the novel and its reader is unique, and will be duplicated by no other means of communication.

One must concede that it is no longer enough to seek out striking facts and events worthy of narrating. The public is supplied more abundantly and massively with such matters from other sources. For some years now real life has been presenting every imaginable subject more impressively than fiction ever could. Readers, moreover, do not seem interested in having their pity and fear aroused. Their curiosity has grown more scientific and is less easily satisfied; they want to see right through everything, and are not so much interested in the facts of a given case as in how these facts came into existence. They are fascinated by the characters' moves, points of view, and shadings of opinion, and the climax comes when they suddenly recognize the intent and are aroused to delighted approval or to anger and resistance—or to both, alternately.

This will be the inevitable result in the novel, because the novel does not deal with a single, restricted situation, with the impression of a moment, or with a permutable, irresponsible impulse; the novel takes the world as its subject matter, or at least a section of it—the very same world in which both the author and his reader live and move. By giving form to this world the author interferes in it, and there are various opinions about the nature of this interference. The discussions about *littérature engagée* are less lively than before, because the concept has not proved amenable to confinement within limits. After the last war cries for a *littérature engagée* resounded loudly everywhere. Above all, the writer was supposed to prove his worth by his "concern," that is, by his attachment to some cause.

The reasons underlying the demand were obvious, all too

obvious. One calls to mind the well-known passage in a poem of
Bert Brecht's stating that "a conversation about trees is nearly
a crime"; [3] for the beauties of nature are irrelevant at a time
when the prime subject is the wrongs existing in this guilt-ridden
world. In Germany the new postwar literature was faced with
the urgent necessity of "conquering the past," as it was frequently called. There were various proposals, some of them
rather ill defined, about how this conquest might be achieved;
but the subject matter lay clearly and distinctly before everyone's eyes: How did it all happen? Where in the past should
the beginnings be sought? What were the possibilities for a future recurrence? What explanation was there for a country
that not only submitted to a deception but also went to war
to defend that deception? Why were great numbers of its
intelligent citizens so blind, negligent, cowardly, and opportun-
istic as to advance the cause of darkness? The kindest thing one
could say of these people was that they failed to show resistance at the right time and so lost their chance to prevent
the evil. How could this nation dare to show its face again
knowing that so many crimes, deeds of violence, and mass
murders had been committed in its name? "Conquest of the
past" did not mean the recovery of lost pride, but acquisition
of certainty that the Germans were thoroughly rid of those
ideas and thought patterns which had made them, in the eyes
of the world, a nation of murderers. As was right and proper,
doubts about whether the evil past had truly been repudiated, or
whether it still lurked under the surface, were not easily or
swiftly dispelled. Then came economic prosperity, the so-called

---

[3] [The reference is to a poem entitled "An die Nachgeborenen," containing
the lines:

> Was sind das für Zeiten, wo
> Ein Gespräch über Bäume fast ein Verbrechen ist
> Weil es ein Schweigen über so viele Untaten einschließt!

Bertolt Brecht, *Hundert Gedichte* (Berlin: Aufbau, 1958), p. 305.

Compare Gorky's statement: "How can one talk about beautiful flowers when
students are beaten by Cossack troops?" Quoted by Irwin Weil, *Gorky* (New
York: Random House, 1966), pp. 9–10.—Translator.]

Wirtschaftswunder, with its unfortunate side effects: the intoxication of quickly amassed riches, stupid arrogance, self-deception, and the persuasive feeling that the Nazi period really had not been so bad as it was painted. Thus past and present joined in the creation of a cycle of themes crying out for literary treatment.

It was said, and justly said, that the whole of this subject matter needed to be frankly and fearlessly exposed to the light of day and analyzed. Whether the author were to write about it for immediate consumption only, or for posterity, would be of secondary importance; above all let these burning issues be brought before the public! The legitimacy and the necessity of purpose in such writing was taken for granted. Still, the novel-form has continued to present numerous difficulties. For one thing, it rather abhors facts—not because facts cannot be adequately expressed in words, but because facts do not lend themselves easily to artistic formation. The author can manipulate fictitious figures according to his wishes and the needs of his work; these figures are his creatures. But when the preservation of historical reality is his purpose, he finds that documented truth and artistic requirements often do not jibe. A kind of natural repulsion or reciprocal antagonism exists between the facts and their utilization in art. It rarely happens that outstanding historical events and personages become the subject matter of equally outstanding works of art; and conversely, the reality of an art work of fictional content may surpass in its vividness the reality of a comparable real-life occurrence. A discrepancy almost invariably results when factual truth and artistic truth are expected to coincide. Facts are less malleable than a subject matter ought to be, if artistic form is the goal; and art, if reduced to a mere medium for the transmission of facts, loses its autonomy.

To speak of artistic truth is not the same as arguing for the artist's right to his notorious "ivory tower." How can one trace an exact dividing line between pure art and that which is *engagé?* To me, every work of art seems to be more or less *engagé.* Of course, the manner in which this "engagement"

is expressed can vary. Anyone who writes or paints or pursues
any artistic endeavor has to be more attentive than other people.
The world is not just his place to work and amuse himself,
not just an arena where he would like to make his mark and
has to make his living; the world is his *material*, and he is en-
gulfed by it. His desire is to analyze this material, which on the
other hand is penetrating him. Because of his sensitivity and
vulnerability he is hit harder and affected more deeply by
people, occurrences, and vicissitudes that the active man reacts
to differently. The active man copes with the world by acting;
the artist by capturing it in forms. His responses, his sym-
pathies and antagonisms, his complaints and judgments will show
up in his work, possibly even when he is only (to hark back to
Brecht's poem) talking about trees. In the process reference
to current events can also of course be included, as may be illustrated with an example taken from the plastic arts: When
Goya was creating his series of etchings entitled "Desastres
de la Guerra" he was preoccupied with the very real events of
his own time. In some of these pictures we see the uniforms
of various French troop units represented with meticulous accuracy. Goya's contemporaries may have been affected in a
special way by the documentary correctness of these uniforms;
later generations, however, would have remained insensitive to
the propagandistic, antiwar significance of the pictures if Goya
had been *only* a careful recorder of uniforms, and not a great
artist as well. The details of uniforms are no great advantage to
the works of art, and might even be considered a detriment
to their quality of universality. But the powerful complaint and
accusation emerging from the whole carries over into every
epoch, and touches and concerns everyone who beholds the
pictures.

The process may also include a desire to promote some cause
or to effect some reform, although experience teaches that this
desire by itself cannot produce a work of art, because it provides too narrow a basis and (literally) a too slanted one. The
mention of Spain above brings Hemingway, about whose "engagement" while writing his novel of the Spanish civil war,

a century later, there can be no doubt. In his novel he does not conceal which side he favors and which of the two warring worlds he deems worthy of defending; nevertheless, he is aware that there are human beings on *both* sides, and makes us see them. Thus a great novel comes into being. In contrast, most of the war novels that appeared after the Second World War strike the reader as inadequate, especially if he himself was an eyewitness to the events, because the writers are so eager to proclaim their horror of the war. While this eagerness is quite legitimate and understandable, it results in representations of the facts that are basically neither better nor truer than the former Nazi propaganda stories. The prinked-up heroes of the latter were all white; the villains of the former are all black. Here is the real danger in a work prompted by missionary zeal: the whole thing must be aimed at demonstration of the purpose with the greatest possible impact. The personages behave predictably, and the plot follows the course expected by the reader. While that may fill him with satisfaction, it will also eventually evoke a sceptical feeling, and he will become vaguely suspicious of the way everything seems to have happened so smoothly and transparently. Smoothness, which in "pure" art results from the artist's uncommitted independence, is here the result of something directly opposite: insinuation and special pleading. In the final analysis, however, smoothness is always sterile. Truths, even poetic truths, are usually rough textured. Hence, though no plan of attack be evident, there is always an implicit challenge in a work of art. It damages itself when it takes extraneous matters into account and allies itself with some cause. The work of art should proclaim, "This is how things are; like it or not, you must hear about it."

The writer's truth! Discovering it remains his greatest difficulty. As he works, he is constantly asking himself, "Can I *say* this or that?" and then, "Can I say it in this way?" Fundamentally the two questions are one.

Let us consider the traditional novel, say the German *Bildungsroman* of the nineteenth century, and the situation of its typical author—presumably an enviable situation. The world

of this novel is explicable and operates according to laws that
are universally assumed to exist, even though they are not
understood in all details. The hero, designed to please cultured
readers, is himself cultured or in the process of becoming so.
At the very least, he must be convinced that culture and matu-
rity in manners and morals are goals worth striving for. From
time to time he may go astray and seem to stand isolated, but
actually he is never forsaken by an unseen guiding power, and
there are always wise persons of superior station to take a hand
in his affairs at the right moment; in dire emergency, help is
invariably near. The omniscient narrator lets the reader participate in his omniscience, so that the reader never loses confidence,
however much the vicissitudes which befall the hero may arouse
his pity.

This happy state of affairs is a thing of the past. Nowadays
the narrator is self-effacing and no longer knows everything.
The individual written about is an obscure figure moving around
in an obscure, confusing world. Generally speaking, he is bound
by his predispositions and entanglements in society and will
make the ironclad claim that he is a "man of no qualities"
(Musil); he may have no personality, or feel an urge to change
his identity (Frisch); or he may be an abnormal person, a dwarf
(Grass). A total tectonic upheaval has occurred, and all we
have left is the negative hero—not negative in the sense of the
tragic Don Quixote, but in the sense that he is entirely lacking
in perception or else is excessively perceptive, hence either not
able or not willing to participate in life. He may be a deserter
from the army, a swindler cheating his way from place to place,
a clown making jokes, or a three-year-old (in size, not in experience!) screeching his protests. Both the well-ordered cosmos
and the human being's central position therein have been lost,
and therefore it is really not possible anymore to establish
any relationship between individuals and events. No longer can
we recognize or accept any correspondency between the person and his destiny; daimon, or indwelling propensity, cannot
be brought into harmony with Tyche, or external fate. Everything has become interchangeable: The hero revels in designs

for himself, and in actions and encounters, all of which are equally possible and equally phantasmagorical. The author has stopped making positive statements; words characteristically found in titles are "conjectures" (Johnson) and "views" (Johnson, Böll)—and we must keep in mind that the term "views" does not have the connotation of the eighteenth-century term "opinions" (Sterne).[4] No longer can a situation be thoroughly illuminated; only superficial highlighting is possible, and that within the limits of a single perspective. The author has had to relinquish his old vantage point in the tower and has had to adopt a restricted view of his subject; narration thus becomes first-person narration. Simultaneous changes have occurred in narrative technique: the orderly succession of events in time has disappeared. With the general perspective lost and only the actual moment remaining, the ability to survey the entire context, the sources and the outcome of the situation, also departs, for how can the moment contain all of this? Only by means of flashbacks and looks into the future, associated with various phases and different aspects of the narrative, can a kind of insight and summarization be achieved. Occasionally we even find that the narrative breaks off and begins anew. Then changes of perspective are unavoidable: The same set of circumstances, or another set, will be viewed from the consciousness of a second, third, or more persons. Joyce had used this technique for years; but in Germany his work exercised little influence until after the war, at which time we also became acquainted with Faulkner's *The Sound and the Fury*.

In recent years the *nouveau roman* of the French has made a stronge impression on the younger generation of German writers. Thorough analysis of this complicated phenomenon (which has not yet hardened into a doctrinaire program) would take up too much space; but one feature that can be mentioned is a special optic power, a sharp scrutinizing of the things making up a person's environment. "Pananthropism" is replaced here by very extreme abstinence from psychologizing (Robbe-

---

[4] [A reference to the title *The Life and Opinions of Tristram Shandy, Gent.*— Translator.]

Grillet).[5] Psychological motivation and analysis, once the central task of the novelist, are abandoned. Although one may possibly infer something from the objects with their changes and relative positions, the conclusions one draws were not planned in advance by the author. The relationships of the objects to people and the relationships of the people to each other can only be guessed at. Nothing is simple anymore. It sounds good to say that the beautiful and the true are always simple—but experience does not necessarily bear this out. Truth, certainly, can be fraught with many difficulties.

I have more than one reason for calling the writer's truth difficult. A storyteller can give form only to what he himself has encountered in life, and only for this can he be held responsible. "Encounter" does not necessarily mean being an actual eyewitness or participant, but it does mean having a significant experience with something and possibly comprehending it deeply. There is a proverb in German which states that he who gives away more than he has is a rogue. Occasionally a writer is fortunate enough to have his experiences accepted with approval by the public, which finds itself enlightened by them; but more often than not his experiences bring him into conflict with the public. Not only does he have trouble finding and transmitting his particular truth, but this truth also gets him into external difficulties. Most writers are glad to revise their work if they themselves see a need for revision; but, failing this, they will certainly not act on anyone else's verdict of true or false, however impressively documented. The author will hardly make the ridiculously pretentious assertion that he is writing *the* truth. But he will want to make sure that he is writing *truly*.

Although not strictly detachable from the broader complex of thinking and apprehension, the author's main consideration is still verbal realization. What are the available means? What can be accomplished? Once upon a time there was something

[5] [See Alain Robbe-Grillet, *Pour un nouveau roman* (Paris: Editions de Minuit, 1963). A statement pertinent to Dr. Gaiser's text is, for example, "Le culte exclusif de 'l'humain' a fait place à une prise de conscience plus vaste, moins anthropocentriste" (p. 28)—Translator.]

called "beautiful language"—one spoke of a "beautiful style." But for modern authors these terms are meaningless. The concept of the beautiful has somehow slipped from our grasp. We still have the word, of course, but are embarrassed to use it except ironically. The concept of the beautiful implies agreement on some norm of beauty; it is associated with idealization. When the old accepted formulas have lost their living content, however, one can attain neither reality with them nor truth. The classical German novel had built up a' bank balance, as it were, and left an inheritance which supported the bourgeois novel well into the present century: a fully developed language, with all the necessary differential characteristics—still fresh, not yet worn out or ossified. This language allowed the individual author sufficient room for free action, but it kept to a definite norm. It was able to supply every need, and the user could always count on being understood. The author's circle—the so-called cultured classes, of which he himself was a member—held its forms and concepts of life in common; it expected him to use the approved elegant language, for this constituted its own ideal. One other possibility also existed: one could be a "popular author," that is, either a naive, untutored genius or someone who had changed linguistic costumes to reach the uncultured readers, the so-called "folk." And the "language of the common man" was also, in a certain sense, right at hand for ready use.

The conditions described above are gone. Nowadays, everyone is within reach of the mass communication media, and these employ a generalizing sort of language that is growing progressively less differentiated in respect to specific needs and capacities. If a language is forced to become all-inclusive; if its terms and expressions are bandied about rapidly within a society whose external homogeneity cloaks a multitude of inner divergencies; then the ideas which are associated with the words inevitably grow more inexact, colorless, and even contradictory. An ever increasing number of words can now mean whatever one likes, and finally lose their meaning entirely, while they go on being used. Such words are similar to currency that has been taken off the gold standard and allowed to rush headlong into inflation.

The individual word no longer adheres firmly to its object, and the whole language shifts and flaps like a loose garment around its concepts and ideas.

Not only are words being emptied of meaning; they themselves are wearing out. The rate of word erosion is accelerating as the speed of circulation mounts. A word, or a clever turn of phrase, which only last year was new and fashionable, may this year already have gone stale.

A similar attrition is observable in musical forms and in the media of plastic arts. This has always gone on, but certainly it has greatly increased in velocity now. The factor of wear and tear is not independently responsible, but in association with changes of consciousness. Where works of art exhibit strong constancy and unquestionable continuity in their contents, there the form is also apt to remain taut and living. For example, religious texts never age, as long as belief remains intact. Should consciousness change, however, atrophy sets in at once. Disruption of continuity makes us ever impatient for something new; but it is one thing to demand the new and another thing to know how to treat it. Let me illustrate once again with an example from the plastic arts: Liebermann successfully painted Dutch net menders; but how can the phenomenon of modern industrial labor be captured with the media of painting? Or: how can one give expression to the day of the modern taxi driver with a linguistic substance harking back to the epoch of the postilion? Obviously, one cannot, except perhaps by recourse to the devices of parody. These matters will be treated more extensively further on.

In the early postwar years, when literature was just beginning again, the phrase "deforestation of the language" *(Kahlschlag der Sprache)* was coined. It was used by that *tabula rasa* generation which was resolved to look upon its time as a "year zero" and to lay completely new foundations for literature. That meant razing the old monuments first. Language had been robbed of its value by misuse and was to be revised. Of course, the first target for destruction was the whole vocabulary of the National Socialist government, that "dictionary of monsters," as it was called in one characteristic title.[6] But distrust went deeper and spread farther than this. It had been linguistic deception on the one side and careless credulity on the other that had led to the inhuman Nazi rule. Accordingly, the ax was sharpened for any term that could serve any kind of irrational idea, for example: all words relating to the area under the general rubric of *Gemüt* (an untranslatable German word),[7] the whole vocabulary of poetic euphemisms that had veiled, palliated, and glossed over enormities; and whatever words offered shelter against the necessary revolution of the German consciousness. Kafka was probably the first truly influential discovery made by this generation; his ascetic style of language became its model. The old elevated tone, as well as the tone of feeling and pathos, had been misused beyond the point of salvaging; moreover, the modern attitude toward life could not be expressed in them. Mere decoration in language, whether justly or unjustly judged to be so, grew suspect; the adjective, for example, was felt to need close inspection because it so often tends to be superfluous or false. The trend toward understatement has continued to be strong. It is noticeable even in the subtitles of novels, subtitles in which a break with the traditional view of the genre's poetic character is implicit; instead of "novel" the term used is "report," "notes," "papers," or "record."

The younger generation had been deprived of any access to foreign literatures, and the contact of the older generation with these had been interrupted. Well remembered is the tremendous urge we felt to catch up with things, the effort that we made to reopen our communications with the world. The Anglo-Saxon literatures commanded our attention first, and a wave of enthusiasm for Hemingway accompanied the broad revival of Kafka. Thomas Wolfe was read a great deal, but the character of his work made imitation too difficult. Faulkner fascinated a rather

[6] [A reference to a series called "Aus dem Wörterbuch des Unmenschen" (prepared by D. Sternberger, G. Storz, and W. E. Süskind), which appeared regularly in the first three volumes (1945–1946, 1947, and 1948) of *Die Wandlung.*—Translator.]

[7] [Approximately, "spirit" or "disposition."—Translator.]

select literary public and exerted a strong influence (as is detect-
able in Uwe Johnson, for instance). Hemingway enjoyed the
most universal success, however. The quality which particularly
intrigued and satisfied us in him was the coolness of his narrative style, and his skillful understatement, which did not exclude
an occasional spare sort of lyricism. Primarily significant at this
point are the new vistas opened by Hemingway to the language
of the novel. It was a revelation to see that he could use collo-
quial language and produce effects no longer possible with
literary language. He brought new vigor and scope to our ideas
of the possibilities inherent in language. The work of James
Joyce, which had already been favorably received by the older
generation (e.g., Döblin), now for the first time could exert
its effect on the younger generation. His techniques of playing
with language and of alternating the levels of language and
vocabulary, his way of letting the linguistic structure enjoy an
autonomous self-realization—all this was accepted and imitated
with new appreciation. It was true that the older novel had also
incorporated borrowings from dialect and the speech of the
lower classes; but these appeared between quotation marks and
were used only as a kind of seasoning to add zest to the story.
Now, however, such elements gained their full accreditation as
the flesh and bones of the general text, as a real part of the
novel's substance: the language of the taverns and the black
market, soldiers' slang, the jargon of construction workers and
of automobile mechanics. Admittedly, these features also contained a certain hint of parody.

It was through parody that Thomas Mann coaxed forth a
last sunset brilliance from the old literary language, humanistic
German. His sovereign irony—which, to borrow Friedrich
Schlegel's familiar words, "surveys everything, rising to infinity
above all bonds, even beyond his own art, virtue or genius" [8]—
expressed, through the medium of irony, a decadent era's consciousness. Parody is to be found in the chronicle style of
Doktor Faustus—a work that is already half a parody by virtue

[8][See the forty-second *Lyceum-Fragment.*—Translator.]

of its revival of an old traditional motif—and in the tirades of Felix Krull, the confidence man.

In *Lotte in Weimar*, an ironically reverential excursion into the classical Weimar period, Thomas Mann added fragments of actual, documented utterances to the fictitious conversations of the characters. This is a technique now called "prefabrication" by the younger generation of authors, who have brought it up to date. Just as in the plastic arts "ready-made" parts are incorporated to produce shock or to express irony, so in narrative texts one will find a passage from an encyclopedia, a court record, a military or hospital report, a newspaper notice, or an advertisement.

The atmosphere of the laboratory pervades modern narrative prose as it does the other arts. The analytical drive expresses itself in various types of experimentation. Authors' energies are taken up with the "how" of the linguistic form and with the principles of structure. Precise linguistic analysis has had its effect on the texts, which are prepared perfectly, as though they were the products of a scientific process. We do not hear, as in the days when consciousness took a different attitude, of the text being "sent out," "proffered," or "bestowed"; instead, it is "submitted" like a scientific record or the report of an experiment. Modern critics often call attention to the high professional quality of texts written by novice authors. There is hardly a vulnerable spot to be found in the linguistic structure, not a trace of the unevenness and rough spots, of the awkwardness, lack of balance, and overenthusiasm that one accepts as the characteristic mistakes of beginners and looks upon with indulgence, perhaps even with sympathy. Evidently there is no room left for naive geniuses. The *poeta doctus* demanded by our technical world cannot operate without his technical apparatus. Hardly any author publishing today is without advanced university training.

Machines, the science of electronics, have also been pressed into service, and not merely for arranging data and making tests, but actually for composing. Linguistic experiments have generally been most common in lyric poetry. The shorter prose forms

have also lent themselves to a procedure whereby language
becomes an end in itself and is more devoted to its own development than to supporting a narrative. The novel, however, has
been less able to overcome its traditional character. Yet there
has been some discussion of a "novel without narrative." For
the time being, any such development remains quite problem-
atical—and possibly with this we have added to the already existing reasons why the novel is sometimes looked on askance, as a
hybrid form of art. Hybrid or not, and in spite of all the
symptoms indicating that it is undergoing a crisis, the novel
keeps on surviving perennially. Its wide acceptance proves that
it meets some need and that people expect to get something
from it. What do they expect? How may they be satisfied?

Artists sometimes brood about the loneliness of the circumstances under which they work; they may even say to themselves that they have no country and are not supported by a
people. But if we apply these laments to our own German situation, they take on a special meaning. Not only are we a severely
beaten nation—so severely that it is practically impossible to
utter the word "German" except in a linguistic sense—but we
are also a nation torn asunder. History records other cases of
this kind, and it would not be so intolerable, provided that the
separated parts lived under similar conditions. The separation
extends even to language. While our connections with the other
literatures in the German language, the Austrian and the Swiss,
have not been severed, there is a distinct danger that one day
two *German* literatures, foreign to each other, will exist. The
regulated languages of officialdom already contain some identical
words which on this side may mean one thing, on that side
another or even an opposite thing. Wider areas may also soon
be affected. Meanwhile, authors on both sides see all too clearly
how they might well have something to say to all Germans, and
they want to say it, in spite of all the difficulties and external
political hindrances. Attempts at an exchange have indeed in
recent years grown stronger and more effective. The great
theme of separation, which is not of political significance alone
but includes a prodigious amount of purely human perplexity

as well, has been treated repeatedly by Uwe Johnson in his novels. Johnson once said of himself that he stands neither on one side of the "wall of infamy" nor on the other, but on top of it.[9] Novels from the other Germany are arriving in increasing numbers in the West. The recently deceased Johannes Bobrowski had his greatest success as a novelist in the West; he too, belonged to both sides.

Among the subjects discussed above was the necessity of coming to terms with the past. It is also necessary to come to terms with the present. Both problems, to be sure, are related. The writer recognizes his task and is disturbed by it. A much debated topic is whether writers can, by literary works, change the world. Obviously, every party and every group urges them to try for such an effect—to the extent that the party or group can itself be served. Skeptics will object that the world is more likely to change the writers. It is a moot point. Words often prove to be ineffective against the pressure of facts and power, but equally often they have, in the last analysis, been victorious, or have caused a long-delayed and unexpected reaction. Thus the writer can probably legitimately assume that he is able to bring about a change. Whether this would be a change for the good or the bad is a matter for his own conscience. He is responsible for whatever change occurs, and cannot escape this responsibility.

Foreign critics have often reproached German novelists, to say nothing of the German people, for concentrating on their own excessively narrow circle and for their self-pity. This criticism is not without basis in fact. But while the German attitude cannot be precisely defended, at least there is a ready explanation for it: the severely wounded consciousness of these authors and their years of isolation from the rest of the world. But, when one considers some of these questions that German novelists seem to have treated in a very restricted frame of reference, do they not actually concern the rest of the world, too? "Provincial" is a term of censure which sometimes comes

[9] The statement was reported in a newspaper account of a discussion with Uwe Johnson.

too easily to our lips. There is certain provincialism about great
cities, also, and even, if I may be permitted the paradox, about
the person who is at home everywhere. It is the *intensity* of a
given work, not its lack of provincialism, that makes all the
difference. Moreover, there is progressively less individuality
about the problems which occur in our more and more uniform
world. The freedom of one is in part the freedom of all, and
the sickness of one, to an extent, affects the health of everyone else. Faulkner has also been accused of provincialism; but
I doubt that the problems he treats would be regarded as specifically American by a German reader. The localities and the
nuances are different, but the human situations are more or less
familiar.

Artists, even though they are given recognition and honors,
are frequently subject to the fear that their words have proved
impotent and their spirit is being ignored. To understand this
feeling we must come back to the artist's position in society,
as seen from another viewpoint. There is that in his nature
which predisposes him to solitude or at any rate makes frequent periods of solitude mandatory. But he often experiences
periods when he detests his loneliness and equates it with a lack
of effectiveness. His reaction then is to adopt a defiant attitude toward society. Characteristically in German narrative
prose of the nineteenth century (and of the twentieth century!)
we find that the main personages stand on the sidelines of life,
that they are queer ducks and intelligent fools, or loafers, or
handicapped individuals; and the author tacitly commends them
for not accepting the world or for being rejected by it. Perhaps
by free choice, perhaps not, they have adopted a resigned attitude. They take refuge in some corner to sulk, or they stand
on some siding, or they pursue some kind of "simple life." A
certain criticism and a passive opposition are implicit in these
figures, and the implicit meaning was caught even then by the
more sensitive ears. Recommendation of an irregular form of
life could also be inferred from these texts. In sum, there was
more than a trace in all this of the concept of the poet as a

person coming "from a far distance" (to use Schiller's phrase[10]). Such "visitors" do not contend with the world, but speak from the sidelines. Of course, the view from the sidelines may provide many a revelation. The dilemma that has arisen between the artist and the real participant in life is at once vexing and productive; and perhaps it is unsolvable.

That there are disadvantages connected with a retreat to the sidelines has been clearly recognized. Modern German writers often discuss this topic in their self-criticisms. We cannot help envying and admiring our neighbor France, where literature holds a central position in society and politics, and the writer traditionally participates in public affairs, indeed is regularly consulted about them. Heretofore nothing similar has occurred in Germany, but now some serious and persevering efforts, at least, are being made in that direction. Social conditions have long been subject matter for narrative literature, which is not to say that they have really been criticized; but the very process of delineation involves the making of distinctions, and to make distinctions is to criticize. But the critic must also be objective and put "distance" between himself and his subject; and the more consistently he does this, the more he tends to adopt an attitude remarkably similar to the position on the sidelines which was deprecated above. On the other hand, critical defiance is aggressive, not resignedly melancholy.

Every society can be called sick in some respects, each has its injustices and falsehoods, each one produces its monstrosities. The sore places have a way of attracting the most attention, inevitably. But if they monopolize *all* the attention, then an inaccurate image results. Let me state the matter simply: If I (speaking as a private individual) look back on my own experience fairly and squarely, I have to admit that in the course of many years I have met a large number, a *quite* respectable number, however, skeptically I apply my judgments, of perceptive, sincere, well-meaning persons. I have seen a good many

10 [The reference is to Schiller's poem "Das Mädchen aus der Fremde."—Translator.]

actions prompted by something besides stupidity, delusion, cowardice, hatefulness, or greed. And I cannot agree that traits loosely called "positive" should always be looked at suspiciously and downgraded for being rooted in conventionality or for emanating from a vain desire to appear good and just. If I turn away from my private life, however, and judge only as a reader of contemporary novels (and not just German novels), I will have to conclude that the world is populated principally by abnormal and monstrous individuals of every description, who act out their miserable lives against a general background of stupidity, sluggishness, and mendacity. Admittedly, everyone has moments of depression in which the world seems to be like that; moreover, it is never easy to say what is normal and what is abnormal. Still we may object that such a dark picture of the world cannot be correct. Here the question of the writer's truth comes up again: The defense will retort immediately, "That is how *I* see it." Are not points of view, however, indicative of more than the observed object? Do they not also indicate something about the observer himself? The author who describes all sorts of undesirable conditions and exhorts against them—is not his own negative feeling to be numbered among these conditions? He is irritated by a pharisaical quality in society—but is not this quality to be found in his own character as well? When a person refuses to see the positive side or deems it beneath his notice, is he not demonstrating thereby a lack of true insight into human life, a certain lack of humor, or even, if I may be permitted the expression, a lack of *love*? Let this stand as a question addressed to modern authors and as a plea for self-criticism on their part.

There are, it is true, certain definite advantages to holding the dark view: Readers find the evil, the crass, and the eccentric automatically interesting. An author can produce effects more readily with such material. Furthermore, experience teaches that less real effort is expended while one is wielding the pen in anger than while guiding it along in a calm frame of mind. There is a morbid attractiveness in stories of catastrophe and decline. It takes less skill to raise gooseflesh on the reader that to raise his spirits—and by that I do not mean merely amusing him. Banal writing is banal writing, whether it purveys candied sweetness or sour depression. It is just as easy to cook up a batch of the one sort as the other, and the sour sells even better than the sweet.

A more serious side of the problem must also be considered: Not only does the unusual in life exert a powerful attraction, but there also seems to be more potential poetic inspiration in the idea of suffering than in the idea of action. I am not speaking of the antihero, for he strives to hold himself aloof and to neutralize suffering. I mean that action becomes more significant and worthy of representation when viewed from the perspective of suffering. Odysseus suffers, and so does Hercules, who does not set about his tasks of his own volition, but is driven and pursued by a malevolent deity that hopes he will perish in the performance of them. Thus the motif is an old one. Literature is intimately associated with a tragic view of the world. Convention alone may be responsible for this, or perhaps convention has been reinforced by repeated experience. In any case, nothing is harder to handle artistically than a happy ending. In Germany, for example, it always smacks of superficiality.

No one can predict whether the tragic view will one day lose its hold. Proverbially, nothing is more difficult to manage than the idyll. In applying this to our own situation, we must not think of the "idyll" in terms of a pretty, restricted little bucolic world. We must imagine a sphere of human existence untroubled by intrusions, crises, and extraordinary occurrences. Material of this nature would indeed prove difficult; but perhaps we dare not bypass it if we are to treat our present world as a whole. Limitations, inescapable routine duties, uniformity, mediocrity, an average amount of good fortune and bad—these, too, are part of the human condition. Whenever new or rare special situations are treated in literature, the critics proclaim that new areas of subject matter have been opened. How seldom does one hear of new areas where ordinary life is concerned! Traditionally, ordinary life is considered a rather unrewarding subject. The only idylls we receive are negative ones. We have had presentations in abundance of the chagrin, vexation, and emptiness inherent in an existence which on the outside appears to enjoy every advantage, being threatened by no danger and satiated with good things. We have been made very well acquainted with the restiveness which is bred by imprisonment in a milieu that one has neither the means nor the vision for changing and bettering. Years ago the peasant and the burgher were regularly depicted in their own proper milieux. The family novel was a standard literary feature, though not regarded as highly as some other kinds of novel. The modern industrial employee, however, and his particular milieu and kind of work, have remained oddly out of reach.

It can hardly be assumed that no one is aware of this subject matter or that it appeals to no one. But here, as always, one needs more than a simple resolve to do something; even a plan of procedure is not enough. Nothing will happen until a certain mysterious stimulus sets the process in motion, a stimulus compounded equally of intuition and artistic understanding. Various epochs have used various terms to designate this stimulus, expressions ranging from "divine fire" to "afflatus" and "frenzy." The term itself counts for little; the important thing is that every author, even the most cerebral type, realizes that the conditions which foster literary condition are extremely precarious. The individual ability to produce can fluctuate uncontrollably: Occasionally it is impossible to start a new work, and occasionally it is incredibly easy. Every author sometimes just has to wait patiently for inspiration to strike him.

Experience further teaches that an expert understanding of the writer's craft, that is, the ability to analyze possibilities, to foresee pitfalls, and to manipulate the apparatus of construction, can be a heavy burden—although at the same time one cannot do without it. This encumbering insight is a concomitant of the author's acquisition of the mature power to summarize. Thus, the best calculations will often result in nothing but unproductiveness. The author expertly visualizes, tests, and *rejects* a plan; as a last step, he may even demonstrate the reasons why such a plan can never be carried out. On the other hand, the factor

which determines action may sometimes arise completely independent of calculation, indeed, in the face of an apparent
impossibility.

We have now returned to the man at his writing desk who
was pictured at the beginning and whose thoughts we have
tried to follow. It seems to me that his situation was prefigured
in an old print that I now want to draw attention to—not that
I am looking for a mere decorative vignette at the end, but because this particular picture so compactly embodies the problems we have touched upon. Old though it is, the print does
not belong to a period altogether different from our own;
again and again it has been called timely and fascinating, and
the perennial interest shown in it is no doubt due to its ambiguous quality and to the perplexing character of its nearly surrealistic configurations. It is Albrecht Dürer's *Melancholia I*,
done in 1514. Much has been written about it. To Dürer and
his contemporaries the state of melancholy was associated with
concentration, with contemplative preparation. We are less
concerned here with historical interpretation, however, than
with what the picture can say to us now. Its main features can
be quickly described:

The picture is dark, literally dark on account of the profusion
and density of its lines and dots. The face of the main figure is
veiled in deep shadows, from which the whites of the eyes
emerge almost startlingly. One narrow section of the picture's
area gives a striking impression of the whole scope of the world:
a patch of sky with a rainbow and a comet, and beneath it sea,
landscape, and human habitations. A vast number of objects are
strewn about, singly or in heaps, in the vicinity of the main
figure: tools of all kinds, altar utensils, implements of time such
as an hourglass and bell, stereometric forms such as polyhedrons
and spheres, a tablet inscribed with number games. There is
also a sleeping dog, and a pot is boiling over a flame. These
objects are for the most part individually explicable, but in combination their relationship to one another remains a mystery. Yet
lack of total understanding does not render the picture meaningless. Everything about it suggests preparation and expectation.

One can almost hear a subdued rustling and stirring. Nothing is moving, however, except the little flame under the pot and the stylus with which a small, really disproportionately small genius is scribbling on a tablet, while crouching with shadowed face on a millstone. What is he writing? Only meaningless signs, perhaps. The massively proportioned, seated woman, gigantic even in this position, lacks all gracefulness; and she is oblivious of the spectator. Brooding deeply and almost as if chained to the spot she sits there, heavily, her head supported on one bulky, clenched fist. Her other hand listlessly holds a pair of compasses, that instrument of exact measurement and planning; it seems to have half slipped from her grasp or else to have been picked up only tentatively. The materials spread around crowd oppressively on her, opportunities for utilization of them are tremendous, all the tools and models are at her fingertips—they cry out to be grasped, so that problems may be solved with them. But as yet, all stands in abeyance.

The man discussed at the outset—he and his work are illustrated in this picture. He wrote his first book with the courage of the novice, his second in the throes of dealing with pros and cons, and in the anguish of doubt. Very probably he wrote his third in defiance of better knowledge and with the courage of desperation. He does not know where he will find the courage to write the fourth, or what kind of courage he needs. But he will not give up without a fight.

The Search for Self, Inner Freedom, and Relatedness in the Novels of Max Frisch

BY CHARLES W. HOFFMANN

The Ohio State University

Four years ago, when Max Frisch's *Andorra* was hailed as the European play of the season and performed with great success on Germany's stages, newspaper critics almost to a man included somewhere in their reviews a note of relief that Frisch had "at long last" returned to the stage. While these reviews were, of course, written by men who make their living writing about the theater, the presumption that Frisch is primarily a dramatist was not theirs alone. The broader public, too, at least until fairly recently, has felt that Frisch's main place is in the theater.

This persistent assumption stems from several things. In his *Tagebuch*, the work that contains the seeds of practically all his later writing and the book to which one must constantly return for the genesis of his thinking, Frisch talks a great deal about the theater, about dramaturgical problems and concerns. Then, too, after his early beginnings in prose Frisch did write exclusively for the theater in the late forties and early fifties, that is, in the years when he first made his mark on the European literary scene. And perhaps most important, critics and literary historians, very much in the habit of mentioning his name in the same breath with that of Friedrich Dürrenmatt, have conditioned their readers to see in Dürrenmatt and Frisch a sort of dramatic Dioscuri, in continual and conscious competition with one another for theatric laurels.

Persistent though it may be, however, the view that the dramatist Frisch is the essential Frisch is, I think, wrong. For one thing, it can be demonstrated—though I do not propose to do so here—that the things which most often claim Frisch's attention are matters better suited to the private world of the introspective novel than to the social world of the stage. *Andorra* is, of course, an exception. Of more obvious importance is the simple fact that, aside from *Andorra* and *Biedermann und die Brandstifter*, Frisch has not written a *new* play since the early fifties.

He has rewritten and revised his earlier dramas, but the mature Frisch has turned increasingly to prose fiction; and in *Stiller, Homo faber*, and *Mein Name sei Gantenbein* he has created three of the most important novels of the past decade. Taken together, these books are perhaps the most meaningful recent German writing in their particular genre: the psychological novel.

Their significance does not lie so much in Frisch's narrative technique. The structure and the plot development in *Stiller* and *Homo faber* are essentially traditional, and only in *Gantenbein* does Frisch move onto experimental, new narrative ground. He has developed a keenly sensitive and often highly imaginative style for illuminating the anguished consciousness of the contemporary intellectual in particular and of contemporary man in general. But while this brilliant style is evident in many single episodes and scenes of each novel, it is not employed consistently in any of the three. The significance of the works lies, rather, in the astonishing accuracy and depth of psychological insight with which the experiences of his typically modern heroes are viewed and presented. His characters are engaged—often against their will and rarely successfully—in what Frisch considers to be the most urgent concerns of living. And while these "urgent concerns" are not profound new discoveries, the psychological understanding that Frisch has for what motivates his characters is rare, indeed. Finally, since most of us can see ourselves in the central figures, the importance of the novels lies also in what they can help us to recognize about our own inner selves. It would be going too far to call Frisch's intent "therapeutic"—but I suspect not *much* too far.

I shall presently define those "urgent concerns of living" in a general way and then subsequently examine in greater detail what each of the three novels has to say about them. First, however, let me make clear that I do not consider the novels to be in any sense a trilogy; and when I compare them to each other I do not mean to imply that Frisch intentionally fills out in one what he left sketchy or incomplete in another. This is not the case. Each novel is unique; and though they sometimes complement each other, as do *Stiller* and *Homo faber* particularly, this is because Frisch tries in each to bring the central character into psychological focus. This is true even for *Gantenbein*, though here the focus never becomes sharp. Obviously *Gantenbein* is a more experimental book than the others and, as such, a novel in which technique becomes important for its own sake. But I cannot agree with the several reviewers who find this work intelligible *only* as a literary experiment and devoid of the instructive implications, the message so clearly present in the two earlier novels. In *Gantenbein*, too, I find Frisch telling us something about man's search for self, about inner freedom, and about human relatedness.

The first concern of Frisch's heroes is the examination of self, and the novels rest on a series of assumptions that Frisch makes (though not always explicitly in the works themselves) about this examination. If man is to develop the ability to live productively with his fellow human beings, he must first look at self. Indeed, until he has done so, he has not even begun to be human, for, though the awareness of self may be what tortures man, it is also the essence of his humanity. Unless he tries to find out what makes him act the way he does, he must remain alienated from self and unfree. One might then expect man to engage willingly in the search for self. But self-discovery is threatening and painful and difficult, while the state of unconscious, alienated, "unfree" living is at least familiar and thus less menacing. It may well be an unpleasant state, but it is also an easy one. Hence, man is not apt to search for his self unless he is forced to do so.

This is more or less the starting point for Frisch's novels. His characters are confronted with circumstances which make the refusal to look at self no longer possible, or at least so threatening that self-examination now becomes the easier path. Each of them has been jarred loose from a familiar and essentially unconscious pattern of behavior by a severe psychic crisis. And since this crisis has been brought on by the old pattern, the character is forced to grant the shortcomings of his previous actions, his previous self, and to search for something better to put in their place. In each of the novels a different phase of this process is examined, and in each different results are achieved.

In *Stiller* the crisis occurred at a time long before the actual narrative begins. In the entries of Stiller's prison diary we are taken back to this earlier time when the final collapse of his spectacularly unsuccessful marriage to Julika, coupled with the failure of his affair with Sibylle, caused him to flee to America. But even before the beginning of the novel Stiller has rejected his earlier self and is apparently well on his way to building a new personality. As we shall see, he fails in this attempt; but of the three heroes—Stiller, Walter Faber, and the narrator in *Gantenbein*—Stiller is the one who searches most diligently, most desperately, and most honestly for self.

In *Homo faber* the hero is not forced to begin his search until the very end of his life, and he dies while still just on the threshold of self-discovery. The book, supposedly a report written by Walter Faber to record the happenings of the preceding three months, once again recounts events and experiences which lie in the past. But here the crisis—which came with Sabeth's death and with Faber's subsequent realization that she was his daughter, that his affair with her has been incestuous—is much closer in time to the actual moment of the narrative. Here the hero is so close to the disaster that he is still overwhelmed by it. The fact that Faber, who has been anything but an introspective person before, now seeks to recall the past in diary form shows that he has begun to examine and even to recognize his self. But in this book Frisch is interested in the mode of behavior that led to the crisis and in his character's immediate response to it. He is not interested in a new orientation, and Walter Faber is given no chance to begin work on a new personality.

In Frisch's most recent novel, *Mein Name sei Gantenbein,* the situation is considerably more complex, though here, too, the starting point is a crisis which seems to have occurred just before the beginning of the narrative and to which the unnamed narrator is reacting. His wife—or was she his lover?—has left him; and, as he stands alone in the tomb that was their apartment, he searches for a self which will fit his state of mind: "Ein Mann hat eine Erfahrung gemacht, jetzt sucht er die Geschichte dazu." [1] As this sentence from the beginning of the book hints, the rest of the novel takes place entirely within the narrator's imagination. He imagines a series of roles, and plays each of them for a while; he creates and assumes a series of hypothetical selves. Sometimes he is the insecure, awkward intellectual Enderlin, sometimes the architect Svoboda; most often he plays his favorite role of Gantenbein, the man who pretends to be blind. All of these roles are merely "rough drafts for a self" ("Entwürfe zu einem Ich"). [2] He tries them on—again in his own words—"as one tries on new clothes." [3] The difficulty is that we are not always sure whether Frisch is creating selves and experiences, any one of which could have led to the *present* state of mind of the narrator, or whether the roles of Gantenbein, Enderlin, and Svoboda are *new* possibilities which the narrator now tries on for size and fit, new selves which he now assumes for a while in the hope of finding a better personality than the one that led to disaster. Though the latter direction is undoubtedly the most important, both are present in the book, and it is often left pretty much up to the reader to take his pick. (Parenthetically, I think we do well, not only in this regard but in others, too, to see Gantenbein as a sort of "do-it-yourself" novel, in which Frisch challenges the reader to put the book together in the way that makes most sense.) At any rate, one thing is clear in this often unclear book: the experimentation with self is so important an issue that it is made to replace story line or plot in the traditional sense.

The search for self is the immediate concern of Frisch's characters, but it is not a final goal. Its value lies in the fact that self-discovery is the necessary prerequisite for achieving inner

---

[1] Max Frisch, *Mein Name sei Gantenbein* (Frankfort: Suhrkamp, 1964), p. 14. "A man has been through an experience, and now he looks for the story to go with it."

[2] Frisch, *Gantenbein*, p. 185.

[3] *Ibid.*, p. 30. "Ich probiere Geschichten an wie Kleider!"

freedom. Unless one comes to know the forces that move him, his actions must remain determined by them. These forces can, of course, be environmental, external; but Frisch's heroes—as I read them—are enslaved by inner forces. The fear of failure, immature dependency, the inability to risk, the need for constant recognition, the dread of whatever is unpredictable, apprehension concerning change, or, on the other hand, the hope for miraculous change—these emotions and others are what keep his characters unfree. Since none of the three heroes come to know self completely, none completely achieves the new orientation of personality, the new character structure which for Frisch is synonymous with inner freedom. None attains the emotional independence which will enable him fully to follow the voice of reason and health and well-being.

All of them, however, eventually look for inner freedom; all come to recognize that they are not free; and all have at least the desire to become so. Again, their success varies in degree. Stiller is the most deeply troubled by his bondage, and in the period that began with his flight from Switzerland and ends with his arrest at the beginning of the novel he has already freed himself of many of his earlier anxieties. "Ich bin nicht Stiller!" [4]— these words, with which the book opens and which are repeated again and again in the hero's prison notebooks, are not just his protest against the discarded identity that society now tries to impose on him once more. They are also his legitimate defense of the measure of liberation he has achieved from his earlier self. During the course of the novel he makes further progress on the road to freedom; and though he is unable to take a last decisive step, his struggle has been a good one.

Unlike Stiller, Walter Faber clings desperately and blindly to his bondage until just before his death at the end of the novel. Actually, it would be more correct to say that inner freedom does not become an issue for him until this time, since Frisch's purpose in *Homo faber* is to sketch a modern, urbane Every-

---

[4] Max Frisch, *Stiller* (Frankfort: Suhrkamp, 1961 [1954]), p. 9. "I am not Stiller!"

man for whom life is both knowable and subject to a set of predictable formulas. For Faber it is simply beyond question that
one can understand and control his experiences according to
preconceived notions of what life is about. It takes a tragedy of
antique Greek proportions to make him see that such living is
not only *hybris* but also slavery to a pattern he has super-
imposed on life and to which he has made his experiences conform. When he finally does recognize, as a result of this tragedy,
that he has been unfree, it is too late for him to do anything
but wish he had lived differently.

In a way, *Mein Name sei Gantenbein* takes up at this point
where *Homo faber* leaves off. The unnamed narrator simply
assumes for himself at the outset the inner freedom that Stiller
struggles to achieve, that Walter Faber merely glimpses; and
the whole novel consists of the uses to which he then puts this
freedom. Or, better, it consists of his experiments in the exercise
of freedom, since his purpose for trying on one role after another
is to find one that will fit the freedom he has assumed. He plays
one identity for a while; but when it leads to boredom or fear or
feelings of guilt—or to some other form of inner bondage—he
rejects it and turns to a different identity to see what its possibilities might be. When being Enderlin becomes threatening
or painful, for example, he switches to the role of Gantenbein.
Or when, as Gantenbein, he tires of pretending that he is blind,
he imagines what would happen if he were now to admit the
deception to his wife Lila. But since this admission soon leads to
difficulty, he puts on Gantenbein's dark glasses again and changes
a different factor in the situation—perhaps Lila should not be an
actress, but a laboratory assistant? or an Italian countess? or a
mother? Though the search for liberation is, thus, very much
an issue in *Mein Name sei Gantenbein*, inner freedom is here
of a quite different order from what it is in *Stiller* and *Homo
faber*. In the earlier novels it is a unique and real orientation
of personality which the character either realizes or fails to realize. In *Gantenbein*—where Frisch does not want to say, "This is
what the character is," but rather, "These are some of the myriad
possibilities the character has within him"—here inner freedom

is something hypothetical, not binding, a field for creative and limitless speculation.

A similar difference between *Gantenbein* and the other works can be seen if we now turn to the third and most urgent "concern of living" to which Frisch addresses himself: the problem of man's relatedness to his fellow human beings. For Frisch the basic condition of man is one of isolation, of existential separateness; and every man seeks to overcome the terrible loneliness of this condition through his contacts with others. But there are healthy ways of trying to overcome isolation, and unhealthy ways, and the real value of self-awareness and inner freedom is that they must come first if the solution is to be healthy. The person who has not tried to recognize and understand what forces motivate his interaction with others must continue to follow these forces blindly. He is not free to consider which of his acts lead to understanding and union and which acts alienate others and lock him in his isolation. If his bondage is extreme, he is imprisoned in a narcissistic aloneness, since everything he does is determined by his own needs and fears and desires. If, on the other hand, a person is completely free, he can look for and cultivate the actions that transcend the self and lead to harmony with others—which is another way of saying that he can love. Most people are at a spot of partial freedom and partial dependency in between these extremes, able to inhibit some of the instincts that block them from the goal but still determined by others.

Frisch's ultimate purpose in all three novels is, in my view, to give new and imaginative expression to this old truth: that men must learn the difficult way of love if they are to escape from loneliness and isolation. Or, to be more precise, his purpose is to show how men fail in the attempt to escape, for Frisch is pessimistic about modern man's chances for success. In all the novels there are only two characters who achieve it, who do learn to love: the district attorney Rolf in *Stiller* and Rolf's wife. Not only are these secondary characters; they also appear in the earliest of the three books. Since then, since 1954, Frisch has not created a character who succeeds. One might perhaps argue for Sabeth, Walter Faber's lover and—as it turns out—his daughter, as an exception. But we see Sabeth only through Faber's eyes, and their witness is unreliable. More important, Sabeth scarcely becomes a character in her own right; her function in the novel is to provide the agency for the Fate that tracks Faber down.

Of the three main characters—Stiller, Faber, and the narrator in *Gantenbein*—none solves the problem of relatedness. To be sure, Stiller, when we first see him at the beginning of the novel, has already come a long way from the narcissistic and thus thoroughly destructive orientation that had once cut him off from his wife, Julika, and from his lover, Sibylle. Both relationships (and particularly his marriage) had been cases of mutual dependency, certainly not of mature love. During his years in America Stiller has come to recognize that this was so and, more important, what he did to make it so. To a large extent he has conquered the feelings of failure and of insufficiency which poisoned those relationships, and now during his imprisonment he also learns he cannot insist that others see him as he wants to be seen. But though he is finally released from his real prison, he is unable to gain complete freedom from the symbolic prison of self. Stiller's new attempt to live in union with Julika is thus doomed, despite his genuine eagerness to make the marriage work this time. To my way of thinking, it is doubtful whether anyone could succeed with so fragile and so withdrawn a woman as Julika, but Frisch holds Stiller himself responsible for the ultimate failure to break out of his isolation.

After showing us in this first novel a character who tries and fails, Frisch shows us in the second a man who never tries. Walter Faber has pretended to escape from the fact of aloneness by shutting his eyes to it. His attempt to live as if life were predictable and readily controlled has forced him to avoid relationships with any real depth to them. Relatedness may be a noble goal; but the search for it involves risk and uncertainty, the necessity of having to choose between values, frustration, and almost certainly some heartache. This makes relatedness too problematic and too complicated to fit into Faber's scheme of things. The contacts he has permitted himself to have with others have been superficial and harmless; and as a result he has only stood on the outside of life. A not very distant relative of Hofmannsthal's Claudio, he has not even looked in until now when death—the premonitions of his own death and then Sabeth's death, for which he is responsible—forces him to do so. As he awaits his cancer operation in the Athens hospital and recalls the events of his existence, he realizes that he has wasted his life. He does not see very clearly why this has happened, but he senses that it is because he never took the critical first step of admitting to himself that he was alone. In *Homo faber* Frisch is thus considerably more pessimistic than he had been in *Stiller* about the chances for breaking out of one's existential isolation.

In *Mein Name sei Gantenbein* he approaches the problem in a different and, again, a conjectural way. Assuming one were not bound to a fixed, real identity but free to experiment with a variety of identities, could he perhaps find a role that would make union with others and the overcoming of separateness possible? To a large extent the novel can, I think, be seen as Frisch's probing for an answer to this implicit question and the constant trying on of identities as a weighing of various possibilities for relating to other people. The fact that the pretended blindness of Gantenbein is the novel's central motif bears out the view that this is Frisch's primary concern. Of all the roles the unnamed narrator tries on, he likes the role of Gantenbein best, because it seems to offer the most opportunities for harmonious living with others. In the role of Svoboda he is almost as unsuccessful in achieving relatedness as Stiller was, and as Enderlin he is only a little more concerned with breaking out of aloneness than was Walter Faber. But as Gantenbein he seems to be able to love creatively, productively; as Gantenbein he seems to come close to finding happiness. Later on we shall see why this is possible, and we shall see also that in the end this happy state of affairs proves to be illusory. Even when the narrator endows one of his imagined selves with the attributes that seem to lead to relatedness, he finds himself unable to escape from isolation.

Thus far I have described some common ground that I find in Frisch's novels. It is now time to leave this general vantage point and to take a closer look at the individual works themselves, or at least at the most important issue in each. Before I do, I should make clear that there are, of course, many other significant concerns in these books in addition to the three I have called central—things like the attack against provincialism or the problem of aging or the disappearance of humane values from an urban and technological world. Very prominent among Frisch's artistic credentials is his inventiveness, and each of these novels is a richly varied texture of themes and motifs. Yet the search for self, the struggle for inner freedom, and the attempt to achieve relatedness remain the heart of the matter.

In *Stiller* the hero never attains freedom or relatedness because he is unable to transcend self, and the crucial point in this failure has not yet been identified. Since Stiller himself never really seems to grasp the point, Frisch does not make it very evident for the reader either, though the situation seems relatively clear until the final section of the novel. Stiller, it will be recalled, had fled to America to escape the utter catastrophe of his earlier life; and in the intervening years he has come to recognize that the catastrophe was largely of his own making. As a result of this self-examination and after an attempt at suicide, Stiller resolved to cast off his old self; and along with the new name of "Mr. White" he has assumed a new and, he hopes, more positive identity. Bit by bit this process is recalled in the prison diaries, especially in the symbolic tall tales with which Stiller so impresses his credulous guard. The most important of these tales are the two in which Stiller describes his exploration of a vast and dangerous cave he had discovered. His hazardous descent was, of course, his descent into himself; and the second time down he managed to save himself only by abandoning a friend whose name was also Jim White—that is, by abandoning his former self.

It is at this point in his development that Stiller is arrested while passing through Switzerland; and the standard interpretation of the novel is that now, during his imprisonment, Stiller is gradually forced to resume his old identity. Julika, his former acquaintances, the state—all refuse to see in the prisoner anyone but the Stiller they once knew, and eventually they compel him to accept their fixed image of him. In this view—its most convincing exponent is Hans Mayer[5]—the book is thus a type of social novel. And its principal message is that society, by making us conform to the image it has of us, forces our lives into repetitive patterns and stifles the wish for change, the attempt to be individual.

While this interpretation is adequate for explaining one aspect of the novel, it runs into serious difficulty on two counts. If applied consistently, it must find the whole last section of the book, Rolf's report on Stiller's life after his release from prison, superfluous. And, more important, it blocks us from seeing that Stiller does not suffer defeat in prison at all. Rather, he is forced here to learn that the attempt to find freedom from his old and unwanted self simply by casting it off and taking on a new personality will not work. Before any real change is possible, he must first go back to where he was. It is not enough just to admit his earlier failures; he must find their causes and, above all, he must accept responsibility for the effects his actions had on others, especially on Julika. Only then can he be released from prison—the prison of his earlier self.

Stiller apparently does achieve this, and when he is finally set free the way seems open for him to begin a new and this time productive life with Julika. Yet, in spite of his desperate willingness to create that life, he fails again; and the key to understanding why is not given until the next-to-the-last page of the novel. Here Rolf looks at Julika, who has died in the tubercular

5 See Hans Mayer, *Dürrenmatt und Frisch; Anmerkungen*. Opuscula aus Wissenschaft und Dichtung, 4 (Pfullingen: Neske, 1963), pp. 38–54, esp. pp. 41–45.

clinic as a result of her operation, and he describes the dead woman by quoting the exact words with which Stiller has described Julika in his diary when she first visited him in prison. Rolf suddenly senses that from the very beginning Stiller has seen Julika as something dead and that, as a result, Stiller's entire relationship with this woman has been a horrendous sin against another human being. Rolf merely states this realization; he does not elaborate on it, and a few sentences later his report comes to an end.

Thus Frisch leaves it to the reader to go back now and re-examine Stiller's life with Julika in the light of Rolf's words. He leaves it to the reader to discover that for Stiller this relationship has been a test case from the outset. A failure as a fighter in the Spanish Civil War, a failure as a lover, a failure as an artist, Stiller had reached the point where he was unable to act except in response to his failures. Everything he did became a new attempt to prove himself, and each new failure led not only to increased anxiety, but also to an ever deepening sense of vague and undefined guilt. In one of the prison notebooks he describes this former self as a "male mimosa," overly sensitive and shrinking from new encounters and new experiences. It was at this stage that Stiller met Julika. First attracted to her because she was too weak to be a threat to him, he saw in her a cold, diffident, completely undeveloped woman—a "crystal fairy," as he later calls her. But he also saw in Julika a woman who might be awakened to love; and, having failed as a sculptor to create in stone and brass, he now set himself the task of breathing life into this shell of a human being. If Stiller had been able to love, this might have worked. But, as it was, the "marriage" soon became the most crushing defeat in Stiller's attempt to prove his *own* worth. As his frustration and anger at this defeat grew, he punished Julika in increasingly cruel ways, finally abandoning her to what he presumed would be her death in Davos.

Of all his previous failings it is his treatment of Julika that has most tortured Stiller during the years of his flight. He has not recognized that his initial purpose had been to bring her to life. But he has seen that in the later days of their marriage he tried to destroy her, and his sense of guilt is so strong that he has accepted responsibility not only for the wish to destroy her but for actually having destroyed her. To be sure, Julika survived her critical illness, but throughout the prison journal Stiller continues to think of himself as her "murderer." And it is in his inability to find a constructive way of dealing with this guilt that Stiller finally fails to transcend self. He is unable to give up the conviction that he once killed the woman with whom he now tries to find a new existence, and this means that once again Stiller seeks Julika—as dead. Only this time he sets himself the still more presumptuous task of bringing her back to life. As a number of motifs suggest—especially the recurrent dream in which Stiller finds stigmata on his hands, or his complaint that he cannot walk on the water—he feels he must perform the miracle of resurrecting Julika from the dead. After failing to be Pygmalion, he tries to be Christ. Of course, he must fail again; Julika dies and, ironically, on Easter Monday.

Frisch thus sets Stiller's ultimate bondage in an implicit religious framework. His purpose is surely not to blame Stiller for being guilty of sacrilege, yet in this religious imagery there is perhaps a final layer of the novel's message. In the figure of Stiller—or so it seems to me—Frisch has drawn an extreme portrait of modern secularized man, unable to believe in any higher instance outside of himself and so forced to take on the role of being his own Saviour. Without an absolute source of strength and direction in which to put his faith, he demands of himself the performance of tasks that men once reserved for gods. And in this sense the novel becomes a demonstration of the psychological disaster—self-idolatry—which has been made possible by man's loss of spiritual belief. Frisch, of course, does not call for a facile return to faith. His portrayal of Stiller is essentially sympathetic, and this means that he wants simply to show how difficult it must be for man to transcend self when self is the only thing in which he can believe.

In Walter Faber, the hero of the next novel, Frisch again paints the portrait of modern man, but this time one who idolizes technology, statistics, machines, "progress." And *Homo faber* is written to show that such idolatry leads, even more clearly than Stiller's self-idolatry does, to psychological catastrophe. It has blocked Faber from all awareness of self, from the chance to become free and to escape from loneliness. The events related in the book now force him to see the error of his living, but recognition comes too late to lead to change. Part of this I have already suggested, but again the crucial point has not yet been isolated and examined.

The point is not, as some have seen it, that Faber's exclusively rational attitude represents such an imbalance that life's irrational forces now take their revenge, tracking him down with the relentlessness of the Furies. This happens, of course, and the clear echoes of Greek tragedy in the book have been well discussed in the critical literature. But to cite them is merely to describe the imagery in which Frisch presents his message; it does not tell us much about the message itself.

Closer to the heart of the matter is the fact that Faber's attempt to live as though life were completely subject to rational control stems from a pervasive fear of life. Afraid of complexity, Faber has tried to force life into a simple pattern. Afraid of chance and accident, he has avoided situations or relationships that might call for an unforeseen response; and whenever unexpected things have happened he has explained them away as mere exceptions to the statistically predictable rule. Afraid of entanglement and disappointment and unhappiness, he has refused to become involved with other people, substituting for true involvement the sort of casual relationship we see in his sex affair with the New York fashion model Ivy. Afraid, in short, of life itself, he has tried to make of it a mechanical process which can be observed and known, but which need not be experienced.

Another way of stating this is to say that Walter Faber is afraid of his emotions, and with this we are getting very near to the unspoken message of the novel. Three years earlier, in one of the prison conversations between Stiller and Rolf, Frisch had described our age as one characterized by a sharp discrep-

ancy between the intellectual development of man and his emotional development. Man has discovered the physical laws that
enable him to master the world around him, but by comparison
his ability to cope with his feelings remains primitive. And the
gap continues to widen, since the more man's intellect develops,
the more adept he becomes at denying his feelings or at deceiv-
ing himself about them. In *Homo faber* this discrepancy is the
central theme. (It might be noted in passing that, like Walter
Faber, several characters from Frisch's dramas can be explained
in terms of a conflict between a highly developed intellect on
the one hand and a stunted capacity to deal with emotions on
the other: Don Juan, the Man of Today ["der Heutige"] in
Die chinesische Mauer, and the teacher Can in *Andorra.*)

The ultimate purpose of *Homo faber* is to suggest the dangers
that face us if this discrepancy is not resolved. On a specific and
explicit level, of course, the dangers are demonstrated in the
story of Faber's destructive love for Sabeth. The very fact that
he is attracted to this girl is the result of feelings with which he
is unable to cope. In the three short weeks just preceding their
meeting on shipboard some very unusual things have happened
to Faber: the crash landing of his airliner in Mexico and the
discovery of his friend Joachim's corpse have made him conscious and vaguely apprehensive of death, and his collapse in the
Houston airport along with the more frequent attacks of his
stomach pains have led to an equally vague realization that he is
beginning to run down, to age. Thoroughly out of practice as he
is, Faber does not examine the feelings these experiences have
aroused, and certainly he does not admit to them. But when he
sees Sabeth in her reddish-blond ponytail and bluejeans, a girl
half his age and still more teenager than woman, he is drawn
to her. He does not see that he is infatuated less with her as a
person than with her youth. But that is just the point. As Hanna
tries to tell him much later, if Faber had been able to recognize
his "love" for Sabeth for what it was—the misdirected attempt to
recapture his own youth—this unlikely and tragic liaison need
never have come about in the first place.

Much more disastrous, however, is Walter's later inability to deal with the feelings he must accept if he acknowledges that he has committed incest with Sabeth. As their trip through France and Italy continues, more and more evidence suggests that she is his daughter (a daughter, to be sure, he did not know he had). But this is so monstrous a coincidence that Faber, accustomed as he is to seeing things in terms of mathematical probability, dismisses it as being statistically all but impossible. Finally, when Sabeth mentions her mother's name, the signs become too obvious to ignore, and Faber reads them. But in the meantime he has slept with Sabeth; and the inner turmoil, the self-reproach, the guilt, toward which the signs also point, are too frightening and too confusing for him to face. Instead he looks for and finds rationally convincing reasons why Sabeth could *not* be his daughter, and this intellectual shutting of his eyes to reality leads to even greater guilt. For instead of trying to cope with the fact of incest, horrendous though it might be, Faber continues with Sabeth the trip which then ends in her death. When this has happened and Faber is compelled to see that he has destroyed not only Sabeth but himself and Hanna as well, the feelings he has failed to reckon with a whole life long take their revenge. They simply overwhelm him, and he stands utterly helpless before the fact of three wrecked lives.

The story of Faber and Sabeth is Frisch's specific example for what happens when man's intellectual development so outstrips his capacity for dealing with his emotions that the latter capacity atrophies. This example alone, however, does not exhaust what Frisch has to say in the novel about the discrepancy. Or better, perhaps: the most sinister implication of the hero's attitude becomes clear when we see his destruction of Sabeth as a sort of symbol. Walter Faber—who, as *homo faber*, stands, of course, for modern technological man in general—is not only afraid of life because it is disorderly and uncontrollable. He also denies life by approaching it as though it were something mechanical. The process of growth disturbs him and that of organic decay he finds obscene. For him the proper study of man is not man, but cybernetics. He not only is attracted to machines rather than to living beings; he also believes that people

are inferior to machines because they are made of less durable
material and are more subject to structural stress. Just as he tries
to treat his emotions as though they were things, so, too, human
beings are things for him. And this means that Walter Faber's
attitude is death oriented, rather than life oriented. He is a destroyer rather than a creator, and for this the destruction of the
daughter he created is a fitting symbol. Walter himself overcomes this orientation in the tragic, but nevertheless *human*
affair with Sabeth. But if it takes a catastrophe of these dimensions to awaken modern man, then the book is a gloomy pre-
diction of where his consciousness is taking him. Narcissism, the
danger in *Stiller*, has been replaced by necrophilia.

The portrait that Frisch paints in his last novel, *Mein Name
sei Gantenbein*, is obviously quite different from the ones we
have seen. It is more complex and more individualized, but
above all it is a composite portrait. It is something like those
Picasso paintings which break up a face into fragments, each
of which is a plane observed from a different angle. Picasso's
artistic intent is to show the subject not as he is seen from just
the front or just the side, but as he appears from various vantage
points at the same time. Frisch's literary portrait is designed
to do something similar: to demonstrate that a person is the
sum not only of a few actual experiences he has had, but also
of all the possible experiences he is capable of imagining.

The form in which Frisch has chosen to realize this intent—the
narrator's experimentation with the various selves he might be—
makes *Mein Name sei Gantenbein* essentially a static book. It
must largely do without the thing that provides the temporal
structure for most novels: plot. Instead, the progression of this
book is associative; one episode gives way to the next when the
narrator tires of the role he is playing or is frustrated by it
and is eager to try on a new role. This means that *when* an
episode begins and ends is even more important than the content
of the episode as such. We learn what moves this unnamed
narrator by examining the selves he imagines, but we learn even

more if we focus on the moments when a role becomes unsatisfactory and a different one is created to take its place. This way of looking at the novel makes it easier to accept the fact that widely divergent and often openly contradictory personalities are united in one character. But it also makes the task of the critic more difficult, and much space would be needed if one were to propose an interpretation for the several hundred moments of association in the novel.

Let it suffice here to say just a few more words about the self to which the narrator returns most often. As I mentioned earlier, of the three main roles he assumes, Enderlin, Svoboda, and Gantenbein, the last is the narrator's favorite because he finds it easier to relate to others when he is behind Gantenbein's dark glasses. In the first place, he gains a number of personal advantages as a result of his supposed blindness. He can win the admiration of others with relative ease—when he somehow seems to "sense" that their wine glasses need filling, for example, or when he beats them at chess, or when he deftly extracts the bones from a trout. He does not have to feign interest in a dull conversation about books he cannot have read or delight with a new dress he does not like. He need take no notice of things that would make him jealous or suspicious or resentful if he had to see them.

Furthermore, being taken for blind makes it unnecessary for Gantenbein himself to react in a number of ways that bring Frisch's other characters to grief. He is released from the urge to teach, to correct the mistakes of the people around him, to reproach them for obvious errors, since it is assumed he cannot see their failings. He can "overlook" shortcomings and mistakes; and when he does so, his partner need not feel that Gantenbein is merely being patronizing. He can do things around the apartment that Lila has forgotten to do, and this does not seem to be a reproach for her neglect. He can pretend not to see the little and the not so little lies that Frisch fears are necessary if people are to live harmoniously with one another. In short, his blindness seems to make it possible for Gantenbein to accept others as they are, to honor the cardinal commandment present in everything Frisch writes: "Du sollst dir kein Bildnis machen." [6] He apparently can avoid Stiller's sin of making an image of his fellow human beings and Faber's folly of making an image of life itself.

Although these possibilities for achieving relatedness are investigated in a number of different situations and with different characters, they are demonstrated primarily in Gantenbein's marriage to Lila. Until late in the novel this imagined union seems to be the happiest and healthiest marriage Frisch has ever described. This, to be sure, is not saying much! But again and again the narrator discovers that as Gantenbein he can love and be loved. And again and again he finds the crucial reason for his success with Lila in the fact that their marriage has room in it for uncertainty, for secrets: "erst das Geheimnis, das ein Mann und ein Weib voreinander hüten, macht sie zum Paar." [7] Gantenbein allows Lila the secret of her lover, whom he sees but pretends to know nothing of; and he believes that Lila allows him the secret of his "blindness," even though she probably suspects the truth. As long as these secrets are kept, Lila and Gantenbein cannot know each other so completely that all uncertainty, all wonder, all surprise disappear from their lives. These things are the magic that keeps their marriage from settling into boredom.

Indeed, for Frisch they are the magic that *any* human relationship needs if it is to remain vital, and precisely for this reason *Mein Name sei Gantenbein* is in the end another pessimistic appraisal of man's attempt to achieve relatedness. For the narrator eventually sees that the feigned blindness of his Gantenbein self might enable him to retain the magic that slips from him when he is Enderlin or Svoboda. But he also acknowledges that Gantenbein's deception leads *away from*, not toward the union and the true understanding which are the goals of relatedness. He tries to find a way to give up the deception, to

---

[6] "Make yourself no graven images."

[7] Frisch, *Gantenbein*, p. 159. "A man and a woman do not become a couple until they have a secret to keep from each other."

have Gantenbein face and accept the reality he has pretended not to see. But though he can imagine two completely different ways for Gantenbein to tell Lila the truth, the result is the same in both instances: the moment he admits he can see, the magic is gone and with it his imaginary happiness. The way Gantenbein has chosen to escape from separateness has from the first been inconsistent with the goal, for Gantenbein has tried to overcome isolation—by isolating himself.

It is, of course, impossible to know where Max Frisch will go now after this brilliant demonstration in *Mein Name sei Gantenbein* of the apparently insoluble dilemma of man's relatedness: that to love, one must be blind, but to be blind to others is to be alone. It is idle to try to guess what his next portrait of man will look like. But we can be reasonably confident that there will be another portrait, for surely we have not heard the last from Frisch on our search for self, on our struggle to be free, and on our one hope for escaping loneliness: love.

Günter Grass
The Artist as Satirist

BY HENRY HATFIELD

Harvard University

Of the many new writers who emerged in Germany after the nightmare ended in 1945, Günter Grass is one of the most talented—a writer with a spectacular flair for language, image, and metaphor. Grass's international renown is based on his prose fiction, but he has written lyrics and a number of plays and dramatic sketches as well. This essay cannot deal with these works—still less with his achievements in the graphic arts and sculpture, or as a jazz musician, though something makes one suspect that he plays a hot—or should one now say a cool?—drum. Rather, I shall confine myself to his two long novels, *Die Blechtrommel* (1959) and *Hundejahre* (1963), with a few words about his intervening story *Katz und Maus*.

In all these works Danzig and the surrounding region, including the rivers and the Baltic, play an important part. As a native of the Free City, Grass regards Germany with a certain distance; he is a semioutsider who betrays no desire to be inside the establishment. His attitude toward Poland and the Polish element in the former Free City is warm and sympathetic. As Grass puts it in his brief poem "Nächtliches Stadion":

> Einsam stand der Dichter im Tor,
> doch der Schiedsrichter pfiff: Abseits—[1]

the poet stands apart—off side.

Born in 1927, shortly before Hitler became a formidable threat, Grass was twelve when the Nazis took over Danzig; later he became—no doubt unwillingly—a member of the Hitler Youth. He was drafted at seventeen, was wounded the following year, and, relatively fortunate, was taken prisoner by the Americans. Released in 1946, he tried his hand at various jobs, then became a student of art, particularly of sculpture. Around 1955

[1] Quoted by Kurt Lothar Tank, *Günter Grass* (Berlin: Luchterhand, 1965), p. 15. "Nocturnal Stadium: The poet stood, solitary, at the goal/ but the referee whistled, 'Off-side'—"

he emerged as a promising writer; four years later *Die Blech-trommel* made him famous.

Strikingly original though they are, Grass's works are in-debted to many literary predecessors. He has mentioned Döblin, Unamuno, Büchner, Kleist, Melville, and Jean Paul, among others. I would venture the guess that he learned also from Grimmels-hausen, Joyce (at least through Döblin), and Thomas Mann.

It would be pointless to tell again the career of the gifted dwarf Oskar Matzerath before, during, and after the Second World War. *Die Blechtrommel* has been called a picaresque novel, a *Bildungsroman*, and sheer pornography. In a famous account of modern German literature, Grass's style is described as "naturalistic . . . with an alloy of surrealist gags," as "the at-tempt at a 'black' literature in Germany." [2] I should like to approach his novels primarily as satires; and to begin by con-sidering *Die Blechtrommel* from the points of view of folklore, of myth, and above all of literature. Certainly it is a work of linguistic art—*ein sprachliches Kunstwerk*.

Oskar's small stature is so central in the narrative that one inevitably thinks of dwarfs—in Wagner, in Barlach's *Der tote Tag*, and especially in Germanic folklore. Of course, we must not forget that he became a dwarf through his own voluntary act, and that he does grow a bit larger later, though he becomes only a very small hunchback; he does not seem to want to attain normality in an abnormal world.

By consulting the standard encyclopedia of German super-stition, one can learn quite a bit about dwarfs, cobolds, and drums, and some of it seems very relevant to Oskar. Dwarfs, one reads, are often as small as children of one, two, three, and four; they are grown up at three years of age. While Oskar is atypical in having a youngish face and no beard, he does wear, in Herr Grass's own drawing for the jacket, the characteristic pointed cap, and his eyes shine bright, which is also typical. Dwarfs are especially fond of music; they often play the drum; their voices, like those of cobolds, are often piercing—*dünn und schreiend.*

---

[2] Albert Soergel and Curt Hohoff, *Dichtung und Dichter der Zeit* (Düssel-dorf: Bagel, 1961–1963), II, 826. [Translation by Professor Hatfield—Ed.]

Since male dwarfs tend to want children larger than themselves, they often seek the love of beautiful human maidens, who sometimes comply gladly. (Oskar, we recall, is the presumable father of a normal son.) Drums, furthermore, are often used for exorcisms, and their sound may prophesy that war is imminent.

More significant than these details is the fact that dwarfs are very ambiguous creatures, often malicious, often beneficent. Some have the evil eye, some help with the housework. Above all, they are both inferior to normal humans and yet, as possessors of magic powers, superior to them. This, I submit, is very close to the concept of the artist familiar in German literature from Goethe's *Tasso* to our own time.

Basically, I believe, the grotesque gnome Oskar Matzerath is an artist, and, as such, mainly a satirist. People cannot resist the magic rhythms of his drum: he has the effect of a bizarre Orpheus; his spell is more powerful, though less sinister, than that of the magician Cipolla in Thomas Mann's *Mario und der Zauberer*. Further, his own voice has telekinetic power: Especially when he is kept from playing his beloved drum, he lets loose with a voice—

. . . that enabled me to sing in so high-pitched and sustained a vibrato, to sing-scream so piercingly that no one dared to take away the drum that was destroying his eardrums; for when the drum was taken away from me, I screamed, and when I screamed, valuable articles burst into bits: I had the gift of shattering glass with my singing . . .[3]

Thus Oskar not only can enrapture the masses, he also can destroy and sabotage, and often does. Sometimes he acts out of sheer mischief: satire for satire's sake, as it were. Yet in his major performance he destroys, or at least ridicules, the meretricious and the corrupt. In a polemical description of Irving Babbitt, H. L. Mencken once claimed that he could make out the chin of Calvin behind the beard of Plato. Is it too much to

[3] Günter Grass, *The Tin Drum*, trans. Ralph Manheim (New York: Pantheon Books, a Division of Random House, Inc., 1961), p. 64 [hereafter quoted as *D*].

sense that behind the blue-eyed mask of Oskar is the half-concealed face of Günter Grass, the greatest German satirist of his generation, who did not hesitate to let loose his far-darting arrows against Bertolt Brecht himself? Not coincidentally, one of the major characters of *Hundejahre* is an artist, too: Eddie Amsel, the creator of grotesque artifacts which serve as scarecrows.

Oskar's far-reaching voice makes one think of Apollo; and it should be no surprise that the dwarf combines, in his own scurrilous way, Apollonian and Dionysiac aspects. Needless to say, Grass's use of mythological allusions is not highfalutin, nor is it obvious, but it is there. For one thing, a writer apparently familiar with Joyce's work as well as familiar with Mann's would not be likely to eschew the employment of myth completely. Moreover, after Nietzsche's *The Birth of Tragedy*, it has become a cliché, at least in Germany, that the true artist or poet must possess both the classic clarity of Apollo and the intoxicating emotional appeal of Dionysus. In Apollo, Nietzsche created a symbol of absolute form; in Dionysus he symbolized the appeal to the unconscious, the anonymous element in man. Both can be dangerous. At one point we read that Oskar "negotiated simultaneously with his gods Dionysus and Apollo." [4]

As the destroyer of shams, conventions, or anything else that annoys him, Oskar Matzerath is pretty clearly a miniature Apollo. As we know from the *Iliad*, Apollo, when angry, is formidable indeed: he slaughters his victims from afar. No one understood this aspect of Apollonian art better than Thomas Mann, who took that god's emblems—the bow, the arrow, and the lyre—as his own. In his brief essay "Bilse und ich" he admits that a writer inevitably wounds the humans he takes as models for his fiction, even though that may be very far from his intention: "The expression which strikes the mark *(der treffende Ausdruck)* always gives the effect of hostility. The well-chosen word hurts." [5] Similarly, Oskar directs the music of his drum,

[4] *D*, p. 323.
[5] Thomas Mann, *Gesammelte Werke* (Frankfort: Fischer, 1960), X, 21. [Translation by Professor Hatfield—Ed.]

or his piercing voice, against anyone who has incurred his anger or disapproval—whether it be a relative, a schoolteacher, or a particularly unpleasant Nazi. Only images of Jesus and of the Dove prove invulnerable, but Oskar is annoyed rather than religiously moved by this circumstance.

His greatest feat, however, is a Dionysiac one. He refuses to join the spectators in front of a grandstand where the Nazis are about to stage a political demonstration, for his friend Bebra has told him that "people like us" -artists, that is—belong *on* the grandstand, not in front of it. But typically he approaches it from behind—seeing its seamy side, as it were—and then takes advantage of his tiny stature to slip underneath the stands, drum and all. Here he deliberately sabotages the celebration by striking up "The Beautiful Blue Danube" from his hiding place. There is loud laughter; many of the spectators join in. The color blue suffuses the whole place, Grass tells us; the nationalistic songs of the brown shirts are driven away. When the Nazi leaders (Grass uses their actual names) approach the speakers' stand, Oskar strikes up even bluer music, a Charleston, "Jimmy the Tiger." All the spectators begin to dance; the occasion is ruined, from the Nazi point of view; but the squads of SA and SS men sent to look for Socialist or Communist saboteurs never suspect that a whistling three-year-old child is the culprit.

Since Oskar's drum is apparently only a toy, few people take it seriously: he is an artist among philistines. Yet it does attract attention. Ironically, Hitler, the invisible villain of the novel whom Grass alludes to as "Heaven's gas man"—one thinks of Eugene O'Neill's iceman—was known for years before he came to power as *der Trommler*—the drummer. In Oskar's hands the drum loses its military aura and becomes an instrument for producing hot jazz—"Jimmy the Tiger," and so on—first in Danzig, finally, after the war, as a member of "The Rhine River Three," a trio playing in a Düsseldorf night club.

To return briefly to the mythical level: Oskar is associated also with Hermes, the god of rogues. The dwarf functions as a picaresque hero or antihero as well as a satirist. Like Hermes, he can be mischievous, even malicious, but he is not really malig-

nant. He refers to himself as "the little demigod of the thieves" [6]
and says elsewhere that Mercury blessed him. He, like his literary ancestor Felix Krull, has the strongly phallic aspect attrib-
uted to Mercury.

A few further points may help to establish Oskar as an artist.
In his account of how he kept the grownups from interfering
with his playing, he uses the technical term for aesthetic distance—*Distanz*. Late in the book he meets a model, whom he
calls his muse. He has a strong affinity with the painter Lankes,
whom he met during the war. Both of them are concerned to
transform their harsh experiences "into the pure, resounding
gold of the postwar period": [7] the artist must live.

Whatever his vices, Oskar's cynicism is not central to his
character: he is basically concerned with finding and expressing
the truth. We recall that at the age of three he deliberately arranged the accident which made him a dwarf for life. Better to
remain an outsider, a grotesque cripple, than to grow into a
philistine or a Nazi. In fact, there is a hint that Oskar's eventual
hospitalization corresponds to his own preference: he would
rather retreat into a metaphorical hermit's cell than be involved
in the teeming but to him boring activity of the Federal Republic. He finds the atmosphere of postwar West Germany "Biedermeier."

Oskar's acquaintance Lankes characterizes the mood of the
Nazi years as "mystic, barbaric, bored." [8] The dwarf himself
disclaims any connection with the resistance or the so-called
inner emigration. To be sure, he helps a gang of adolescents perform acts of sabotage in Danzig during a blackout, but this is
not presented as a political act. Oskar expressly says that he had
aesthetic reasons for opposition: he disliked the color and the
cut of Nazi uniforms, as well as the Nazi music. In *Die Blechtrommel* the satiric tone is largely comic, at least on the surface.
Fiercer attacks were reserved for Grass's second novel, *Hunde-*

[6] *D*, p. 130.
[7] *D*, p. 551.
[8] *D*, p. 337.

jahre. Yet Oskar scores sharply when he describes a Rhinelander who always "screamed, laughed, and clapped" [9] when others did; and accordingly became a Nazi out of sheer conformism. When he refers to a German cannon as "a virgin of the clan of Krupp," [10] one is reminded of Erich Kästner's political verses.

To turn to *Die Blechtrommel* as a verbal work of art: one may best characterize it, I believe, as baroque. This long, rich book is full of the violent contrasts, the extreme tensions which we generally ascribe to that style. Thus Oskar associates himself, as Mr. Erhard Friedrichsmayer has shown, with the infant Jesus, in a more or less blasphemous parody.[11] While there are scenes and images of great beauty—like the evocation of the January night in the chapter "Show Windows"—the language inevitably tends toward the grotesque. Of course, Oskar's presence alone would account for that; his love affairs are particularly *outré*. Grass is addicted to picturing eels in a remarkably repulsive way, and his descriptions of vomit are almost literally emetic. His sense of death and evil underlying life resembles that of the seventeenth century or the late middle ages. At the very end of the book a sinister black cook is evoked; she seems to symbolize guilt, and may remind us of the black spider in Gotthelf's novella of that name. For all his sense of comedy and wit, Oskar is whistling—or rather drumming—in the dark.

On a more cheerful note, one observes that Grass has a sheer joy in words which is comparable to Rabelais' or Joyce's—or, for that matter, to Heimito von Doderer's. I would venture to suggest that Doderer is the more pleasant—at his best he is delightful—Grass the more "far-out," radical, and incisive; though at least one of the symbols (the octopus) in Doderer's *Die Dämonen* is drastic enough to have been created by Grass. A striking example of Grass's verbal gusto occurs in his description of the impact of the German bombardment on the defenders of

---

[9] *D*, p. 152.
[10] *D*, p. 232.
[11] Erhard Friedrichsmayer, "Aspects of Myth, Parody, and Obscenity in Günter Grass' *Die Blechtrommel* and *Katz und Maus*," *The Germanic Review*, XL, iii (1965), 240–250.

the Danzig post office. He operates here with great skill, making his effect by cumulative parallelism, a strong rhythm, and alliteration:

> ... there came a whirring as of angels' wings, a singing as of the ether singing over the radio. It didn't hit Bronski, no, it hit Kobyella, Lord, what a sense of humor that projectile had: bricks laughed themselves into splinters and splinters into dust, plaster turned into flour, wood found its ax, the whole silly nursery hopped on one foot.[12]

As one might expect, Grass delights in playing with words. Describing an imaginary geometrical figure which came to his mind while looking at a snapshot, Oskar relates: "I spun out projections . . . described arcs which . . . provided a point, because I needed a point, a point of vantage, a point of departure, a point of contact, a point of view." [13] The use of two contrasting modes of narration—third person as well as first[14]—adds to the richness of the novel.

Symbolic images abound. The Nazi grandstand, hollow, completely unimpressive once one gets behind it, comes to mind. When the hopelessly outnumbered Poles are surrounded in the Danzig post office, one of them builds an elaborate house of cards. Oskar's curiously mixed nature is illustrated by his two favorite books: a volume of Goethe and a cheap thriller about Rasputin. During the war Oskar and other members of a troupe of performers organized to entertain the *Wehrmacht* act out an

[12] *D*, pp. 233–234. The effects mentioned are more noticeable, of course, in the original German: ". . . da klirrte es, wie vielleicht Engel zur Ehre Gottes klirren, da sang es, wie im Radio der Äther singt, da traf es nicht den Bronski, da traf es Kobyella, da hatte sich eine Granate einen Riesenspaß erlaubt, da lachten Ziegel sich zu Splitt, Scherben zu Staub, Putz wurde Mehl, Holz fand sein Beil, da hüpfte das ganze komische Kinderzimmer auf einem Bein . . ." Günter Grass, *Die Blechtrommel* (Berlin: Luchterhand, 1959), p. 283.

[13] *D*, p. 55. Again, the original German text shows the particular feature of style more markedly: ". . . es kam zu Parallelverschiebungen . . . zu Zirkelschlägen die . . . einen Punkt ergaben, weil ich einen Punkt suchte, punktgläubig, punktsüchtig, Anhaltspunkt, Ausgangspunkt, wenn nicht sogar den Standpunkt erstrebte." Grass, *Blechtrommel*, p. 60.

[14] Pointed out by Grass himself in an interview with Professor Burton Pike, which is scheduled to appear in the *Paris Review*.

absurd little drama with some soldiers guarding the Atlantic Wall in Normandy. It is the eve of the invasion; concrete bunkers are everywhere, but the soldiers, as the actors, have had enough of martial life, of mysticism, barbarism, and boredom. Already they are dreaming of the prosperous Biedermeier period after the war, complete with bowling alleys, turtle doves, and refrigerators.

One other tension should be mentioned: that between a cynicism extraordinary even in our day and a certain paradoxical faith in man—an absurd humanism, if you will. (Perhaps some day some bold fellow will note an analogy between *Die Blechtrommel* and *Doktor Faustus*, though this would probably annoy both Herr Grass and the revered shade of Thomas Mann.) There is no point in amassing examples of Grass's cynical wit: as someone said of Wagner's leitmotifs, you can't possibly miss them. Quite aside from the erotic bits and the association of Oskar with Jesus, there are dozens of touches like the remark about the pieces of stone from bombed-out buildings which were "resurrected," as Grass puts it, to mark the graves of the dead—"if one can say such a thing about gravestones"; [15] or the designation of homosexuals as the "male mistresses" [16] of their protectors. Yet the humanistic note is still heard: Oskar admires Goethe, even though he realizes that the admiration would not be mutual; and something tells him that the Nazis could never win the war, "even if they succeeded in occupying Alaska and Tibet, the Easter Islands and Jerusalem." [17] He defines "human" *(menschlich)* as "childlike, curious, complex, and amoral." [18] His definition tells us a great deal about himself, and about Grass's reasons for choosing a grotesque little drummer as his hero.

In its title, *Katz und Maus* (1961), Grass's novella recalls the cat-and-mouse situation typical of Kleist's dramas: the pro-

[15] Grass, *Blechtrommel*, p. 544. [Passage translated by Professor Hatfield, omitted in *D.*—Ed.]
[16] *D*, p. 523.
[17] *D*, p. 241.
[18] *D*, p. 80.

tagonist, like the Prince of Homburg or Alkmene, is cruelly played with by a stronger power (or person), though he may eventually fight his way to salvation. Further, a central symbol of the novella is the Adam's apple of the protagonist Joachim Mahlke, which happens to be exceptionally prominent. Now it is hardly a coincidence that the myth of Adam and Eve also plays a great part in Kleist's writing and thought, as in *Der zerbrochene Krug, Käthchen von Heilbronn,* and his important essay on marionettes. Grass mentioned Kleist as one of the authors to whom he is most indebted, and I believe that the interwoven motifs of cat and mouse and Adam's apple provide the key to Grass's story. In the first paragraph of *Katz und Maus* one of his school fellows encourages a young cat to leap at Mahlke's twitching Adam's apple while he lies resting, apparently asleep; and the characteristic motifs recur consistently.

To return to the action of the novella: it, too, is set at the time of the Second World War. Joachim Mahlke is an unusual youth, extremely brave, ambitious to a fault, and rather grotesque in appearance. He is tall and very thin, with an embarrassingly large Adam's apple. (German schoolboys, I am told, believe that this protuberance is an index to the sexual powers of its possessor.) Although the actually highly sexed Mahlke is the most chaste of the group, the familiar association of apple, sin, and sex is clearly established. In any case, his Adam's apple stamps the protagonist as a marked man. His extraordinary devotion to the Virgin Mary further sets him apart from his anything but pious comrades.

Mahlke first demonstrates his bravery by feats of swimming and diving; he saves one boy from drowning. With his companions, he likes to spend time on the projecting deck of a small Polish warship sunk not far from Danzig. It is the "island" to which they escape from an irksome world, though their pastimes and conversations are not of the sort recorded in the *Swiss Family Robinson* or *Die Insel Felsenburg.* Mahlke is the only one who can dive well enough to penetrate inside the ship to a cabin which is still free of water. He makes it his shrine, and there he tries to take refuge from the Army authorities at the end of the novella.

First, however, he has a military career of his own. It has an inauspicious background: Mahlke incurred disgrace by stealing the decoration of a U-boat officer who was visiting his school. As this insigne—the "Knight's Cross of the Iron Cross" —was worn around the neck of its holder, it more than outbalances any Adam's apple, however unaesthetic, and irresistibly attracts the boy. After voluntarily confessing his sin, he is relegated to another Gymnasium, and soon volunteers for war service. With his tense devotion to duty, he manages to destroy so many Russian tanks that he is himself awarded the Knight's Cross. Returned to Danzig on leave, however, he is cruelly snubbed by the director of his original school, who refuses to let him address his former classes, as the U-boat officer had done. This catalyzes Mahlke's discontents with society: he deliberately misses the troop-train back to the front, gives rein to his long-suppressed sexual drives for one night only, beats up the director with the help of his friend the narrator, and throws away his decoration. Hoping, or seeming to hope, to desert to a neutral country, he goes back with the narrator of the novella to the sunken ship. There he disappears and presumably dies. There is a strong hint of suicide.

One notes that Grass has "distanced" the story by making a personal defeat, not some Nazi crime, the occasion of Mahlke's defection. It is nevertheless, I believe, a moral parable. Joachim Mahlke is a person of quite exceptional will power and courage. He also has more than his share of the "old Adam," but generally he keeps it in check: normally, he is downright ascetic. Here, of course, his devotion to the Virgin is relevant. His greatest strength—and weakness—is his extraordinarily competitive spirit. He is as focused on performance as any of Mann's "heroes of creative work"—the *Leistungsethiker*. Typically, the appeal to his competitiveness is responsible for his only indulgence in one of the less attractive forms of adolescent sexual play. An obscurely sensed ambition also leads him to steal the officer's decoration. Clear now about his own motives, he can win a cross of his own. In his eagerness to blot out his disgrace by appearing at his old school, he is abnormally sensitive: The director's refusal amounts to the end of his career. Fate, or the era, is playing a cat-and-mouse game with him.

Symbolically seen, the Knight's Cross represents to Mahlke a talisman, in fact a sort of "anti-apple," which makes the embarrassing "apple" or "mouse" on his own throat irrelevant. When, however, he realizes that the way of life represented by that decoration is false, he throws it—and presumably his life— away. By so doing he saves his soul—to use an expression which Herr Grass would probably find painfully old-fashioned or even superstitious. Yet he is the most admirable person in Grass's fiction, and the narrator—as Grass himself noted[19]—is impelled by a persistent guilt complex to write about his friend. We have no way of knowing whether the mouse Mahlke would have survived in a time when the cats were less cruel and vicious. There is one hint: he would have liked to be a clown, but the warlike mood of the period blocked that avenue of ambition.

Mentioning clowns reminds one that Oskar Matzerath appears several times, as does the unpleasant Tulla Pokriefke, who plays an important part in *Hundejahre*. These carry-overs seem interesting, and recall Grass's statement that he would like to devote a number of novels to the Danzig scene. Clearly, he is gifted enough to become the Balzac or Dickens of the erstwhile Free City; but one must point out that Danzig is neither Paris nor London. Fortunately, however, he also describes the Rhineland and a genuinely free city—Berlin.

Equally ambitious and almost equally as long as *Die Blechtrommel*, *Hundejahre* is darker in tone than its predecessors. It treats the same period, and its action takes place largely in the same areas: the territory of the Free City and the Rhineland. In fact, Oskar and his drum are mentioned several times. Its overall structure is more complex; there are three sections: "Frühschichten" (Morning Shifts), the ironically entitled "Lie-

[19] See Kurt Lothar Tank, *Günter Grass* (Berlin: Luchterhand, 1965), p. 77.

besbriefe" (Love Letters), and "Materniaden" (Materniads), each with its own narrator.

The other side of the coin, however, is that *Hundejahre* is less sharply focused than its predecessor. For one thing, the dog, or rather the succession of dogs, is not so potent a centralizing symbol as is Oskar with his drum—and, with all respect for dogs, I must say that the dwarf is much more interesting than they. The second novel is harsher and less distanced than *Die Blechtrommel*. At times the satire is heavy-handed, as in the account of the rumors circulated about Hitler's dog Prince after the *Führer's* inglorious demise. Yet *Hundejahre* is a rewarding, many-faceted, and important book.

To deal first with the implications of the title: "Dog Years" seems to denote the twentieth century. The third narrator, Matern, exclaims: "O ye dog years hoarse from howling!" [20] Possibly it is relevant that in the dog *days* men tend to be moonstruck, and dogs to go mad. Many or most of the generation that Grass portrays are doglike in their blind, often stupid obedience. A poor wretch is an *armer Hund* (poor dog), and *Du Hund!* (you dog!) is a crass insult. One may recall Erich Kästner's lines—"Hier liegt ein Teil des Hunds begraben auf den ein Volk gekommen ist" [21]—in other words, the German nation has gone to the dogs. Hitler's weakness for German shepherd dogs is well known, and the Nazis were generally far kinder to animals than to people. When Harras, the father of the handsome dog which was given to Hitler, becomes vicious, Matern calls him "Nazi."

The basic plot of *Hundejahre* is relatively simple: we read of boys growing up in and around Danzig, of the impact of Hitlerism and the war, and of the postwar period. Perhaps the most interesting figure is Walter Matern, who protects his

[20] Günter Grass, *Dog Years*, trans. Ralph Manheim (New York: Harcourt, Brace & World, 1965), p. 503 [hereafter quoted as *Y*].

[21] "Here lie buried parts of the dogs this nation has gone to." From "Inschrift auf einem sächsisch-preussischen Grenzstein" in Erich Kästner, *Gesang zwischen den Stühlen* (Stuttgart: Deutsche Verlags-Anstalt, 1932), p. 37. All rights reserved by the publishing house of Kiepenheuer and Witsch, Cologne.

gifted, half-Jewish friend Eddie Amsel from bullies, but later betrays him. After the war Matern, filled with guilt and anger, takes grotesque revenge on all the former Nazis he can reach. Amazingly enough, Eddie Amsel survives; he reappears in the third part as "Gold Mouth": Nazi bullies, including his ambivalent friend Matern, have knocked all his teeth out.

The most striking aspect of the book is Grass's phenomenal virtuosity of style. Adroitly rotating his narrators, and repeatedly shifting the time of the narration from around 1960 to the days before the war and back again, Grass revels in parody, puns, and other Joycean devices. His repeated parodies of Martin Heidegger are fierce, but not, I think, unjust: the weird jargon of the Freiburg philosopher figures as a kind of double talk which serves to conceal or evade reality. He is one of the former Nazis on whom Matern takes vengeance, calling him by such epithets as "ontic dog," "pre-Socratic Nazi-dog". I will not quote many of these passages, for it is almost impossible to translate Heidegger into German, let alone English. Thus the capitalized words, "ICH, GRUND, GRÜNDEND IM AB-GRUND!" [22] are not much clarified when rendered as "I, GROUND, GROUNDING IN THE GROUNDLESS!" [23] Yet one gets the point when soldiers drafted by the Nazis parrot the phrase, "After all, the essence of being-there is its existence," [24] when rats are described as "the grounds of the ground." [25] when the possibility of a moonless night is expressed by the words, "the moon, in case it should nihilate." [26] In Grass's view Heidegger has corrupted a language, which in turn served to corrupt its speakers.

Hundejahre is full of bravura passages. Thus Grass compares the brown color of Nazi uniforms to dung and continues: ". . . Party brown, SA brown, the brown of all Brown Books, Brown Houses, Braunau brown, Eva Braun, uniform brown, a

[22] Günter Grass, *Hundejahre* (Berlin: Luchterhand, 1963), p. 456.
[23] *Y*, p. 377.
[24] *Y*, p. 298.
[25] *Y*, p. 299.
[26] *Y*, p. 300.

far cry from khaki brown . . ." [27] Twice, emulating Joyce,
Grass constructs catalogs based on the alphabet, as for instance:
"A as in 'away with it' . . . B like 'Bacchanal'—Now let us make
merry. C like 'Cato.'—*Ceterum censeo*, we should kill another
bottle. D as in 'Danzig.'—In the East it was prettier, but in the
West it's better. E for 'Eau de Cologne.'—I tell you, the Rus-
sians guzzle it like water." [28] Some very rhythmical passages
build up the effect of an incantation: "And the Vistula flows,
and the mill mills, and the narrow-gauge railway runs, and the
butter melts, and the milk thickens—put a little sugar on top—
and the spoon stands upright, and the ferry comes over, and the
sun is gone, and the sun returns, and the sea sand passes, and
the sea licks sand . . ." [29] Elsewhere Grass imitates even the
language of birds.

In a surrealistic radio forum, held after the war, Walter
Matern has to discuss his past with a group of young people
who ask him very searching questions. The tone is deceptively
light, parody and black humor abound, a chorus chants doggerel
verses; but the essence is serious. One of the questioners has a
pair of magic spectacles which reveal the past: Matern has no
choice but to tell the truth. Although he claims to have been
morally and politically pure, the sins of his dog years come out,
including his part in the vicious beating of his friend Eddie
Amsel by a Nazi gang. We learn also that he has slept with
Hitler's mistress—or so he claims—and that the black shepherd
dog Pluto—to whom we must return—once was called "Prince"
and belonged to Hitler. The point of this uncanny interlude
would seem to be that the guilt of Matern's generation was all
but universal. Since Matern loathes his past, and tries in his confused way to atone for it, there is hope for him; but he must
live with hideous memories.

Usually exuberant, sometimes excessively wordy, Grass's style

[27] *Y*, p. 196.
[28] Grass, *Hundejahre*, p. 451. [Passage translated by Professor Hatfield, since
the corresponding passage in *Y* is much adapted and altered from the original
text.—Ed.]
[29] *Y*, p. 54.

can be concentrated and nervous. At times, to avoid banality, he breaks off a sentence before its end, leaving the reader to infer the rest. He describes a gypsy as follows: "A man in his middle forties. Pale brown black impudent, hidden behind the bush. Hook-nosed rabbit-eared toothless." [30] Grass is indeed a man of many devices, and at times his verbal arabesques and baroque flourishes obscure the narrative line.

Often fantastic though he is, Grass includes realistic, even naturalistic touches. To re-create the atmosphere of the Danzig region, he brings in local history, mythology, and superstitions. Frequently he has recourse to dialect. He names actual persons and firms: besides Heidegger, he mentions Flick and other industrialists, Rudolf Augstein (the editor of *Der Spiegel*), Siemens Halske, the Ullstein concern, and so on.

Yet, as in *Die Blechtrommel*, it is the major symbols which really take us to the heart of the matter. The first important one arises from Eddie Amsel's hobby of constructing grotesque scarecrows. (The descriptions of these weird artifacts remind one of some of Grass's drawings, like that of the spider which illustrates his poem "Gleisdreieck.") Although Amsel's creations do actually frighten away the birds, they are essentially artistic renderings of his own experiences: he portrays in them people he has met and even records in scarecrow form an incident in which his schoolmates, already anti-Semitic, beat him cruelly. Surrealistic though these unusual mobiles are, they are based on nature: he feels they are part of nature. Amsel's most important constructs, however, are images of SA men—". . . only Tulla[31] and I knew he was making SA men who could march and salute, because they had a mechanism in their bellies. Sometimes we thought we could hear the mechanism. We felt our own bellies, looking for the mechanism inside us: Tulla had one." [32] (Compare Goethe's metaphor for Alba's soldiers, in *Egmont* [Act IV, "Street"]: "machines in which a devil sits.")

[30] *Y*, p. 95.
[31] A particularly unpleasant adolescent girl, who plays a central role in Part II of the novel and also appears in *Katz und Maus*.
[32] *Y*, pp. 205–206.

While the ordinary, obedient Germans appears as dogs, the Nazis are scarecrows, monsters. Amsel also plans to build a giant, Phoenixlike bird which will always burn and give off sparks but never be consumed—a symbol of the creative artist, and perhaps of his own survival.

As the strength of the Nazi movement increases, in the second part, so does the number of swastika flags along the Danzig waterfront. Eventually the war breaks out. The dog motif becomes more important: nasty little Tulla, so called after a mythical figure (her real name is Ursula), repeatedly sets the dog Harras on an inoffensive piano teacher. Prince, the puppy Harras has sired, is trained by the Danzig police and then presented to the *Führer*. For her part, Tulla, shocked by a swimming accident, regresses for a time into sheer animality: she spends a week in Harras' kennel, sleeping there and sharing his rations. Dog years indeed!

As mentioned, the third part of *Hundejahre* is centered on Matern's adventures after the war and his determination to punish the Nazis he knew. Matern is all the more implacable because of his own guilt; in boyhood he was noted for grinding his teeth, and his temper remains fierce. Accompanied by the dog Pluto—the name is appropriate, for postwar Germany is seen as Hades—he travels over the countryside, exacting bizarre revenge on his victims. That he finds most of the culprits' addresses written on the walls of the men's room of the Cologne railway station is in line with the desperate sordidness of the first years after the German surrender. Matern's characteristic revenge is to debauch the wives or the daughters of his guilty acquaintances.

The symbol of the prophetic meal worms—they live in a bag of flour belonging to Matern's father—is of a farcical sort. These worms can foretell the future, so leading industrialists and intellectuals make pilgrimages to the house of old miller Matern, who becomes more and more prosperous as the "economic miracle" continues. Finally the East Germans kidnap the remarkable little animals. All this may seem—or be—excessively farfetched, but I believe that Grass is satirizing a vein of superstition which persists in Germany even today. Even otherwise intelligent people often turn to astrology, for instance.

The most successful symbol in Part III is the magic spectacles which play a decisive part in the radio program described above. These eyeglasses, produced in great quantity by the mineowner Brauxel (who appears as Amsel in Part I of the novel), enable young people to see exactly what their elders did in the Nazi years. Thus when the ten-year-old Walli sees Matern through the spectacles he has just bought her, she screams and runs away—and Matern is by no means the worst of his generation. Such eyeglasses are, indeed, easily available in West Germany today—in accounts of the trials of Eichmann and other criminals, in movies, in dramas such as *The Diary of Anne Frank* or *The Deputy*, and of course in innumerable books. This chasm between the generations could hardly be wider and deeper. It is a bitter but inevitable situation.

Appropriately, the long novel ends with a visit to Amsel-Brauxel's mine—the deep well of the past. The dog Pluto is taken down into the mine, but his name is not changed to Cerberus, for "Orcus is up above," Brauxel says,[33] not beneath the earth's surface. The mine appears as a veritable inferno: Amsel-Brauxel is manufacturing scarecrows again, and his technique has become far more sophisticated. These automata—described as scaffolds and skeletons—are so processed that they can weep, laugh, hate, feel sexual emotion. They are indoctrinated in religion, military skills—and above all in German history. This reads like a dreadful indictment of all Germans, but Grass seems to exempt the younger, post-Nazi generation.

The survivors are more or less reconciled; but memory and isolation remain. After emerging from the mine, each one takes a bath. Matern hears Eddie Amsel whistling in an adjoining cabin. To quote: "I try to whistle something similar. But it's difficult. We're both naked. Each of us bathes by himself." [34]

33 *Y*, p. 561.
34 *Ibid.*

Notes on the Contributors

GERD GAISER has won literary fame as a novelist, short-story writer, and lyric poet. He has won four literary prizes in Germany; his work has been the subject of many critical articles and of a full-length study (by Curt Hohoff, 1962). His collections of short stories are entitled *Zwischenland* (1949), *Einmal und oft* (1956), *Gib Acht in Domokosch* (1959), and *Am Paß Nascondo* (1960). His novels, which have been translated into English and other languages, are *Eine Stimme hebt an* (1950); *Die sterbende Jagd* (1953), a work reflecting its author's experiences as a fighter pilot in World War II; *Das Schiff im Berg* (1955); and, best known of all, *Schlußball* (1958). Dr. Gaiser does not consider himself, however, to be primarily an author; he is a painter and a professor of art at the Pädagogische Hochschule in Reutlingen, Germany.

HENRY HATFIELD is professor of German at Harvard University. Among his numerous publications in fields of research ranging from the eighteenth century to the most recent German literature are four books: *Winckelmann and His German Critics* (1943), *Thomas Mann* (revised edition, 1962), *Goethe: A Critical Introduction* (1963), and *Aesthetic Paganism in German Literature* (1964). In collaboration with F. H. Mautner, Professor Hatfield published *The Lichtenberg Reader* (1959), for which he both selected and translated the texts. From 1947 to 1952 he was general editor of *The Germanic Review*.

CHARLES W. HOFFMANN is professor of German at The Ohio State University. His special scholarly interest is contemporary German and Swiss literature, and he has published critical essays on Hagelstange, Brecht, and others. He is the author of a monograph entitled *Opposition Poetry in Nazi Germany*. While on the faculty of the University of California, Los Angeles, Professor Hoffmann was given official recognition for his distinguished teaching.

HEINZ POLITZER is professor of German at the University of California, Berkeley. He is the author of numerous scholarly articles dealing with various periods of German literature and of the widely discussed book, *Franz Kafka: Parable and Paradox* (1962). A German version of this book was also published. Professor Politzer's collaboration in the years 1935 to 1937 with Max Brod on the first edition of Kafka's collected works forms a unique background for his interest in Kafka. As a creative writer himself, Professor Politzer has published three volumes of lyric poetry and a German translation of Coleridge's *The Ancient Mariner*.

WALTER HERBERT SOKEL is professor of German at Stanford University. A specialist in modern German literature, he has published, in addition to critical essays, a book on Expressionism, *The Writer in Extremis* (1959), and *An Anthology of German Expressionist Drama* (1963). *The Writer in Extremis* appeared also in German translation as *Der literarische Expressionismus*. Professor Sokel's latest major work in his comprehensive book, *Franz Kafka: Tragik und Ironie* (1964).

Index

alienation: theme in Böll's novels, 3, 11; in *Die Blechtrommel*, 5, 122; as a characteristic of Böll's witness-figures, 16–18, 20; in German narrative prose, 84–85; in Frisch's novels, 95. SEE ALSO artist; isolation

Apollo: as related to Oskar in *Die Blechtrommel*, 120

Arendt, Hannah: her *Eichmann in Jerusalem*, 24

artist: as standing apart from life, 5, 84–85; as combining Apollonian and Dionysiac traits, 120

Austria: as "Kakania," 39–40; compared to Germany, 49; rift in political parties of, 54; Doderer's essay on, 55; literature of, 61; and marriages, 62; connections of, with German literature, 82

Babbitt, Irving: described by H. L. Mencken, 119

Balzac, Honoré de: and Paris, 55, 128

Barlach, Ernst: his *Der tote Tag*, 118

Berg, Alban: his music termed "Kakanian," 40

Bildungsroman: as extinct type, 73–74; as designation for *Die Blechtrommel*, 118

Bobrowski, Johannes: success of, in West Germany, 83

Böll, Heinrich: his novels as analyzed by Walter H. Sokel, 3–4, 11–35 *passim;* his characters compared to Oskar in *Die Blechtrommel*, 5; his *Haus ohne Hüter*, 11–13, 14, 16–17, 19, 23–24, 25, 26, 27, 29, 30, 32 (Gäseler, Nella, Rai), 34 (Rai); his *Und sagte kein einziges Wort*, 11,

13, 15, 22, 29, 33; his *Wo warst du, Adam?*, 13–15, 18, 19, 22 (Feinhals, Schniewind), 27, 29, 32, 34 (Ilona); his *Billard um halbzehn*, 13, 14, 16, 18 (Schrella), 19, 21, 22–23, 24, 25 (Robert Fähmel), 26, 27–28 (Heinrich Fähmel), 29 (Heinrich Fähmel), 30, 32 (Robert Fähmel, Hugo, and Nettlinger), 34 (Robert Fähmel); his *Ansichten eines Clowns*, 13, 14, 18, 30–33, 34, 75; his *Brief an einen jungen Katholiken*, 33; his *Doktor Murkes gesammeltes Schweigen*, 34

Bonn Republic: rejected by Böll's witness-figures, 16; Nazis retaining power in, 19

Brecht, Bertolt: his poem "An die Nachgeborenen," 70 and n. 3, 72; satirized by Günter Grass, 120

Broch, Hermann: influence of, on Doderer, 45; views of, on Joyce, 45–46; his *Der Tod des Vergil*, 45, 50–51; distinguished from Doderer, 48; interest of, in words, 49–50

Büchner, Georg: mentioned by Grass as influence, 118

Cain and Abel: as motif in Böll's novel, 21, 31–32

Calvin, John: associated with Irving Babbitt, 119

Catholicism: in Böll's novels, 28-33; Doderer's conversion to, 41; Roth's conversion to, 49

Christianity: as theme in Böll's novels, 19, 20–21, 24, 28, 29–30

"crisis" of the novel: 5, 42, 44–45, 68, 82

Deputy, The (Roth Hochhuth): and the younger generation in Germany, 134

Diary of Anne Frank, The: and the younger generation in Germany, 134

Dickens, Charles: and London, 128

Döblin, Alfred: and James Joyce, 80, 118

Doderer, Heimito von: 3, 41–62 passim; his Die Dämonen as analyzed by Heinz Politzer, 4, 42–62 passim; biography of, 41; his Die Strudlhofstiege, 41; his Tangenten (Diaries), 41, 42, 52; compared to Grass, 123

Don Quixote: distinguished from modern negative hero, 74

Dostoevsky, Fedor M.: as influence on Böll, 15; his The Possessed, 42

Dürer, Albrecht: 89; his Melancholia I as illustrative of situation of the contemporary novelist, 89–90

Dürrenmatt, Friedrich: associated with Max Frisch, 93

dwarf: in connection with Oskar in Die Blechtrommel, 74, 118–119, 122

Eichmann, Adolf: 134

Eisenreich, Herbert: as successor to Doderer, 61

Faulkner, William: as influence on Böll, 11; his The Sound and the Fury, 75; his appeal for German readers, 79–80; his provincialism, 84

Friedrichsmayer, Erhard: his article on Grass, 123 and n. 11

Frisch, Max: 3; his Mein Name sei Gantenbein, 4, 7, 94–95, 96–97, 99–100, 101, 102–103, 110–113; his novels as analyzed by Charles W. Hoffmann, 4, 94–113 passim; his Homo faber, 4 (Walter Faber), 94–95, 96, 98–99, 101–102, 106–110; his Stiller, 4, 94–95, 96, 99, 100, 101 (Julika), 102, 103–106, 107 (Rolf, Stiller), 112 (Stiller); and change of identity, 74; his Biedermann und die Brand-

stifter, 93; his Tagebuch, 93; his Andorra, 93, 108; his Die chinesische Mauer, 108; Don Juan of, 108

Gaiser, Gerd: 3, 5, 6, 65, 135; his Eine Stimme hebt an, 5, 135; his Das Schiff im Berg, 5, 135; his Schlußball, 5, 135; his Die sterbende Jagd, 5, 135

Germany, postwar: activity of, 3, 5; as pictured in Böll's novels, 11–22 passim; Böll's witness-figures surviving in, 16–22; former Nazis in, 20; role of Catholics in, 31; new literature in, 70; Biedermeyer atmosphere in, 122; Danzig in postwar period, 129; seen as Hades in Hundejahre, 133. SEE ALSO Bonn Republic; Nazis

Gide, André: as interpreter of own works, 67; his Paludes, 67 n. 2

Goethe, Johann Wolfgang von: his concept of the artist, 119; his Tasso, 119; as favorite author of Oskar in Die Blechtrommel, 124, 125; his Egmont, 132

Gotthelf, Jeremias: his Die schwarze Spinne, 123

Goya, Francisco de: as artist and propagandist, 72

Grass, Günter: 3, 117–133 passim; his Hundejahre, 5, 6, 117, 120, 122, 128–134; his Die Blechtrommel, 5, 74, 117, 118–125, 128, 129, 132; his novels as analyzed by Henry Hatfield, 5, 117–133; as born storyteller, 69; biography of, 117–118; his Katz und Maus, 117, 125–128; his poem "Gleisdreieck," 132

Grillparzer, Franz: as "Kakanian" writer, 40

Grimmelshausen, Hans Jakob Christoffel von: as influence on Grass, 118

Hatfield, Henry: 5, 135; article by, 115–134

Heidegger, Martin: parodied by Grass in Hundejahre, 130, 132

Hemingway, Ernest: as influence on Böll, 11; writing of, about the Spanish civil war, 72–73; reception of, in Germany after Second World War, 79–80; his language, 80

Hercules: the suffering hero, 87

Hermes: similarity of, to Oskar in *Die Blechtrommel*, 121. SEE ALSO Mercury

Hillen, Gerd: 3

history: used by Doderer, 41, 52, 60; as involving difficulties for the novelist, 71

Hoffman, Charles W.: 4, 135–136; article by, 91–113

Hofmannsthal, Hugo von: on the breakdown of communication, 44–45; his "Letter of Lord Chandos," 44–45, 51; on Prussians and Austrians, 49; his *Andreas*, 49; as viewed by Broch, 51; his poem, "Manche freilich . . .," 57 and n. 29; and the surface of existence, 62

Huysmans, Joris Karl: reminiscence of his *Là-bas*, 42

identity, search for: in Frisch's novels, 4, 95–97

Iliad: 120

inner freedom: as goal in Frisch's novels, 98–100

isolation: 60; of German authors, 83; as basic condition of man, 100–103, 113. SEE ALSO alienation; artist

Jean Paul: as influence on Grass, 118

Jesus Christ: association of Stiller with, 106; image of, resists Oskar in *Die Blechtrommel*, 121; parody of, in *Die Blechtrommel*, 123; association of Oskar with, 123, 125

Jocums, George A.: 3

Johnson, Uwe: use of word "views" by, 75; influence of Faulkner on, 79–80; and the theme of separation of the two Germanies, 82–83

Joyce, James: as influence on Hemingway, Faulkner, and Wolfe, 11; his use of the *Odyssey*, 42; his *Ulysses*, 42, 51; his *Finnegans Wake*, 45; evaluated by Broch, 45–46; distinguished from Doderer, 48; and changes of perspective, 75; as influence on the younger generation in Germany, 80; as influence on Grass, 118, 120, 130; his joy in words, 123

Jünger, Ernst: contrasted with Doderer, 49

Kafka, Franz: as "Kakanian" writer, 39, 40; similarity of, to Doderer, 48; and Prague, 55; his *Der Prozeß*, 55; revival of interest in, 79

Kahn, Robert L.: 3

"Kakania," "Kakanian": and former Habsburg lands and their cultural atmosphere, 4, 39–41, 48, 55, 56, 57; and the affinity for beautiful language, 49–52; negative aspects of, 40–41, 58; Doderer's place in, 60–61, 62

Kästner, Erich: his political verses, 123; his poem "Inschrift auf einem sächsisch-preussischen Grenzstein," 128 and n. 21

Kleist, Heinrich von: as influence on Böll, 33–34; as influence on Grass, 118, 125–126 (*Katz und Maus*)

Kokoschka, Oskar: as "Kakanian" artist, 40

Kraus, Karl: as "Kakanian" writer, 40, 58; his *Die letzten Tage der Menschheit*, 40, 59

language: as used (beautifully) by Doderer and "Kakanian" authors, 48–52, 55; as problem for contemporary novelists, 68, 76–82; as used (ascetically) by Kafka, 79; as used by Grass, 118, 123–125, 130–132

Lehár, Franz: as "Kakanian" composer, 40

Levin, Harry: on Joyce's *Ulysses*, 51

littérature engagée: 69, 71–73

love: in Frisch's novels, 4, 100–103,

108–109, 112–113; in Böll's novels, 15, 32, 33, 34; as lacked by contemporary novelists, 86

Manichaean: element in Böll's novels, 20–21, 24
Mann, Thomas: his linguistic experiments, 42; his *Doktor Faustus*, 42, 51, 80, 125; his *Der Erwählte*, 46; and the "spirit of narration," 46; distinguished from Doderer, 48; his use of parody and "prefabrications," 80–81; his *Lotte in Weimar*, 81; as influence on Grass, 118, 120, 125, 127; his *Mario und der Zauberer*, 119; his "Bilse und ich," 120
Mayer, Hans: and the interpretation of *Stiller*, 104
Melville, Herman: as influence on Grass, 118
Mencken, H. L.: 119
Mercury: as prototype for Oskar in *Die Blechtrommel*, 122. SEE ALSO Hermes
Mommsen, Theodor: 52
moral problems: in Böll's novels, 12–13
Musil, Robert: as "Kakanian" author, 39–41; his *Der Mann ohne Eigenschaften*, 39, 40, 47, 74; and plot in novel, 47, 52, 60; and language, 49–50

"narrator as idea": discussed by Broch, 45–46
Nazis: and Böll's characters, 3, 5, 14–15, 16, 17, 28, 29, 30–31, 34; and Oskar in *Die Blechtrommel*, 5, 121, 122–123, 124, 125; as continuing in power, 19–21, 24–25; regarded as not so bad, 25, 71; in Austria, 41, 59; propagandistic literature of, 73; language of, 78–79; and Danzig, 117; and Joachim Mahlke in *Katz und Maus*, 127; in *Hundejahre*, 129, 130–131, 133, 134
negative hero: in modern novel, 74, 87

Nestroy, Johann: as "Kakanian" author, 40, 62
Niebuhr, Barthold: 52
Nietzsche, Friedrich: on the nature of the artist, 120; his *The Birth of Tragedy*, 120
nouveau roman: influence of, on contemporary German writers, 75

Odysseus: as suffering hero, 87
Odyssey: used by James Joyce, 42
omnipresent narrator: in the "total novel," 4, 46
omniscient narrator: absence of, in Böll, 11; in *Bildungsroman*, 74
O'Neill, Eugene: 121
Orpheus: as prototype of Oskar in *Die Blechtrommel*, 119

parody: 78; as used by Joyce and Mann, 80–81; of Heidegger by Grass, 130; in *Hundejahre*, 130–131
Picasso, Pablo: as analogous to Frisch, 110
Plato: and Irving Babbitt, 119
Politzer, Heinz: 3, 4, 136; article by, 37–62
Protestant: as attitude of Böll's clown, 33
Proust, Marcel: distinguished from Doderer, 48; associated with Doderer, 51
provincialism (parochialism): of Doderer, 4, 54, 62; as problem of German novelists, 83–84; attacked by Frisch, 103
psychological novel: 48, 75–76; as written by Frisch, 94, 95, 107

Rabelais, François: his language compared to Grass's, 123
Railles, Gille de: treated by Huysmans, 42
Raimund, Ferdinand: as "Kakanian" author, 40
Ranke, Leopold von: 52
Rasputin: and Oskar in *Die Blechtrommel*, 124

reality: preoccupation with, in contemporary novels, 6
Robbe-Grillet, Alain: and the *nouveau roman*, 75–76
Romains, Jules: and Paris, 55
romans fleuves: and Doderer, 47
romans mosaïques: and Doderer, 47
Rommel, Erwin: 20
Roth, Joseph: and language of novel, 49; his *Radetzkymarsch,* 49

satire: Grass's view of, 5; in *Hundejahre,* 5, 128, 133; Grass's novels as, 118, 122
satirist: Oskar in *Die Blechtrommel* as, 119–123
Schiele, Egon: as "Kakanian" artist, 40
Schiller, Johann Christoph Friedrich von: attitude of, 4; his poem "Das Mädchen aus der Fremde," 85 and n. 10
Schlegel, Friedrich von: his forty-second *Lyceum-Fragment,* 80 and n. 8
Schnitzler, Arthur: as "Kakanian" author, 40
Schönberg, Arnold: as "Kakanian" composer, 40
separation of the two Germanies: as a theme for the contemporary novel, 82–83
snobbery: as theme in Böll's novels, 25–27, 29, 30, 32
Sokel, Walter Herbert: 3, 136; article by 9–35
Spiegel, Der: mentioned in *Hundejahre,* 132
"spirit of narration": in Thomas Mann, 46
Stein, Gertrude: as influence on Hemingway, Faulkner, and Wolfe, 11

Sterne, Lawrence: 75
stream of consciousness: in Böll's novels, 11
Switzerland: literature of, 6, 82; Stiller and, 98, 104

"total novel": Doderer's concept of, 4, 44–46, 48, 52–53
truth: the writer's concept of, 73, 76, 86

Unamuno, Miguel de: as influence on Grass, 118

vengeance: seen as futile, in Böll's novels, 23–25
Vienna: and Doderer's *Die Dämonen,* 4, 42, 44, 53–54, 55–56, 57–58, 61

Wagner, Richard: and dwarfs, 118; and leitmotifs, 125
Webern, Anton von: as "Kakanian" composer, 40
Willson, A. Leslie: 3
Wirtschaftswunder, das: and Böll's characters, 18, 26; as theme for the novel, 70–71
witness-figures: in Böll's novels, 15–18, 22–23
Wittgenstein, Ludwig: his linguistic mysticism, 51
Wolfe, Thomas: as influence on Böll, 11; acceptance in Germany, 79
World War, Second: its aftermath as theme in novels, 6; in Böll's *Wo warst du, Adam?,* 13–14; and "Kakania," 39, 54; and Doderer, 41; and Vienna, 55; and war novels, 73; and Oskar in *Die Blechtrommel,* 118; and *Katz und Maus,* 126. SEE ALSO Germany, postwar; Nazis; separation of the two Germanies